About the author

Karen Ingram is a mother, feminist, performer, celebrant and activist who has chosen Melbourne, Australia as her home for more than thirty years while remaining connected to her hometown of Newcastle. She has worked in the music biz as artist manager and publicist, and has been an educator, presenter, media spokesperson, counsellor and social justice advocate – collecting experiences like feathers to grow a colourful and majestic boa.

kareningram.com.au

Dedication

Andrew – you have stood by my side and shared the wonder, amazement, shock and sadness of life and supported all of my creations. I could not have done this without you.

My two finest creations, Angus and Brigit – you will always have a place in my heart and in our family history. Connection and belonging to the past and future are yours.

I acknowledge the Awabakal and Worimi people as traditional custodians of the land and waters which grew me and the Wurundjeri and Boonwurrung peoples as traditional custodians of the lands where I grow my family and where I learn, work, love, play and create. I acknowledge the enduring impacts of colonisation on Aboriginal and Torres Strait Islander peoples and the sorrow of the Stolen Generations – past, present and future. Sovereignty has never been ceded.

Praise for this book

I was absolutely riveted and loved it. I was fascinated. And I think any reader would be. — **DOM HARDEN**

A story of belonging and family, it's also partly an ode to growing up in Australia in the 70s. I enjoyed the social commentary and imagining the constraints of the times on the women in the story. — **RG**

After reading Lifting the Lid I have a greater understanding of the plight of those adopted children trying to complete their identities. I've been touched and informed by this story and reminded of childhood and growing up in that era. — **HARRY M**

You have such a distinctive voice and I think that really comes through, without ever swamping the narrative. Your inner struggle, and your integrity and compassion as a human being are so evident and so moving. — **YONI P**

I got out of this story the very real and harrowing story of someone who searched for a missing link. I saw frustration and joy and the depths in between. I got out of the story that the loss of identity is devastating. — **V BRIGHT**

The yearning/searching/finding experiences were much deeper emotionally than my concepts of people finding their birth families. People who love family history will love reading this book! — BEC GELSI

It was beautiful. You have the ability to touch the hearts of those with whom you share this — that's the highest aspiration your art can have. Thank you for making me think about all these things.
— PAUL H

This would make a great movie! — DR TASH

LIFTING THE LID
a memoir born of adoption

KAREN INGRAM

Published in Australia by
Ojoy Media, Melbourne, Australia

kareningram.com.au

© Karen Ingram 2021

All rights reserved. No part of this publication may be reproduced, stored in a retrieval system, or transmitted, in any form or by any means without the prior written permission of the publisher, nor be otherwise circulated in any form of binding or cover other than that in which it is published and without a similar condition being imposed on the subsequent purchaser.

 A catalogue record for this book is available from the National Library of Australia

ISBN: 9780648892007

Front cover photograph by unknown
Back cover photograph by Michael Rosenstein
Cover and text design by Cath Pirret Design
Author photo by Mikaela Egan

Disclaimer
All care has been taken in the preparation of the information herein, but no responsibility can be accepted by the publisher or author for any damages resulting from the misinterpretation of this work.

Prologue

Many people have an adoption story – their own, in their family or their wider circle of friends. While the premise is similar – the separation of babies from birth mothers and their biological truth – the way each story unfolds is unique, just as people, places and time. I've been telling the stories in this book since I can remember, and they've become entrenched in the memory of my heart and mind with each telling. It is beyond time I moved from telling to *showing* what happened on my quest to know the truth about my identity, and sharing why it is important – for everyone.

I decided to lift the lid on stories that would otherwise be forgotten, stories from an innocent childhood in a conservative family, coming of age and becoming the woman I am – while bound and influenced by social policy and pressures throughout the twentieth and twenty-first centuries.

Readers will notice an assortment of styles throughout the different chapters as I merge non-fiction with fiction, mix in verse and imaginings, as well as primary sources such as artefacts and letters.

I have written *Lifting the Lid* in order to claim a space for myself and my children in a lost family history, and to ready ourselves for the future.

Some of the names in *Lifting the Lid* have been changed.

FLYING DREAMS

I'm flying like a bird, in silence
Scanning the rooftops and cliffs
I am strong and in control of my direction
Yet a magnetic connection brings me here
Time and time again

The hang-gliders show me the way
I flirt with risk at the cliff top, my courage grows
Safe above the rooftops, knowing what I know
Crashing waves unstoppable, persisting
More than background noise, it's my soundtrack

I'm at my freest
Soaring high, swooping low without fear
I know I'll return to this familiar place
Where my dreams and reality collide
Time and time again

Who lives down there? How can I be them?
Knowing what I can see, not knowing what I can't
What lies beneath the terracotta rooftops?
The stories, the history, deception and lies
What does it have to do with me?

THE CALL

It's the morning of Tuesday 8 March 1994. I answer the ringing phone.

'Hello?'

'Hello, is that Karen Forbes?'

'Yes, it is.'

'Hello Karen, it's the Post Adoption Resource Centre here in Sydney. Could I just check with you that you were born on the 8th February 1965?'

'Yes, I was.'

My pounding heart is deafening.

'I'm holding a letter written by your birth mother in 1986. Would you like me to read it to you?'

Choking on a tight ball of nerves, I mutter, 'Yes I would, thank you.'

Quickly scrambling for a piece of paper and a pen, I stand at the phone table in the hallway, barely breathing as I hear the words of my mother for the first time.

YOU'RE SPECIAL. WE CHOSE YOU.

Over the years I heard it over and over – like a mantra that I believed completely. One Saturday afternoon when I was about three years old, at a playground waiting for my brother's soccer game to start, Mum gently pushed me on the swing until I gained some rhythm and height. She allowed the momentum to subside and gave me another push.

This was the day she first told me my truth. Standing at my side as I swung back and forth.

'Karen, sweetheart,' she began, 'You know that Mummy loves you very much.'

'Yes,' I replied with all the confidence of a three-year-old who had only ever known enormous love from her mummy and daddy.

'I have something important to tell you,' she continued as I watched the sky open up before me with each push on the swing. 'Before you were born you grew inside another lady, but she wasn't able to keep you after you were born.'

My little mind boggled as I took in her words. It was well before the time when I knew where babies came from, but I had always known that my mum was my mum, always. Without missing a beat, she continued in her warm, wise and caring way. Before I could ask why, Mum explained: 'This lady wasn't able to keep you, but she loved you very much and wanted you to have a happy life with another family – a family who would love you and look after you, always.'

I accepted this new story wholeheartedly. It all sounded completely reasonable and I felt no sadness or bitterness towards the lady who couldn't look after me. I felt lucky because I had no doubt in my mind that my mum and dad and my brothers were my family and that I was definitely where I belonged. Where I belonged.

Many times after this, Mum told me how they'd waited a very long time for me. My two brothers were born ten and twelve years before I came along. There had been another brother too, his name was Mark and he died when he was only a few days old. My parents had their hearts broken. While Mum's emotions are never far from the surface, Dad has always been much quieter, a deep thinker, caring and thoughtful. Mum and Dad endured five miscarriages after the death of Mark, all baby boys. Mum especially yearned for a baby girl. They also discussed their heartache and longing for another child, a baby girl, with their trusted priest. Through church connections, adoption became a real possibility, and in 1958 Mum and Dad's names were put on a waiting list to adopt a baby girl.

My brothers Jeff and Neil were babes of 1950s suburban Australia. Mum and Dad were a typical Anglo-Christian couple who attended the local Church of England regularly and took part in many of the church social events. They both played roles on committees – Dad often as treasurer, Mum as secretary or organiser of volunteers to visit the sick and elderly in their homes, part of the work of the Mothers' Union. Gender roles were entrenched throughout society; the destiny of men and women clearly defined from birth. A young girl went to school until she could gain a good job, where she would remain until she married. At this point she'd leave the family home and her job to live with her husband and take on her new role of looking after her home, her husband, and later, her babies. A young boy went to school and was encouraged to develop interests and learn about areas that would increase his chance of getting a good job – often an apprenticeship or an entry-level position at a large company. Mum and Dad didn't know anyone who had completed their Higher School Certificate (HSC), let alone anyone who went to university.

They both left school with an Intermediate Certificate, today's equivalent of Year 9. Mum secured a good job at the local steelworks, Comsteel, a major employer in Newcastle throughout the best part of the twentieth century. Conveniently, it was in the suburb where she lived with her parents, a brother and a sister – her two older sisters having married and moved out in the post-war boom. Dad also worked at the steelworks as a white-collar worker. Family folklore recounts their first meeting in the pay office. Noisy and crowded, there was always an air of anticipation and expectation as all the staff lined up, slowly edging forward to collect their cash-filled pay envelope. Mum recalls noticing a well-dressed, handsome young man asleep in the window of the pay office on this particular pay day.

After they married, they lived in a house behind the house where Dad grew up. His father managed The Newcastle & Suburban Cooperative Society, commonly known as The Store, in Cardiff and their place was a few streets away. Dad's dad, whom we called 'Poppa', and his brother, Uncle Arnold, built the house for Mum and Dad in the block of land behind. The back fence that separated the newlyweds from my mum's in-laws was made of chicken wire and had a wooden framed gate for easy, regular access. Privacy was nil. Mum wasn't a fan of this arrangement, but she lived there within full visibility of her in-laws for twelve years. This was the house where Mum and Dad had their children – the Forbes family. It was my first home.

While they waited for word on the adoption of a baby girl, they gave their abundant love to their two sons as well as many foster children: some would arrive on weekends and school holidays, others were more irregular. My brothers went to the same public school where Dad had gone, Cardiff Public School, and played soccer at Cardiff Football Club. Mum had a lot to do as a homemaker and church-going volunteer. They didn't have a car in those early days and when they finally did get one, Dad would drive to work. He was steadily advancing within the large company and earned a modest salary to support his wife and children.

On the first Thursday of March in 1965, Dad received a phone call at work. Seven years after being placed on the waiting list, it was the adoption agency calling to check that he and his wife still wanted a baby girl. To Dad's affirmative response they advised him their baby girl would be delivered to them on Monday. This was a huge and very welcome surprise after a seemingly eternal wait.

That evening, Mum stood at the sink peeling potatoes, as she did every evening at this time. Jeff and Neil lay on the lounge room floor watching TV. Dad arrived home from work, as if it was any other ordinary day. With a kiss hello after a long day apart, Dad asked Mum to sit down for a minute.

'I can't sit down now, I've got to get this dinner on.'

'Dinner can wait, love, come and sit down. I have some news.'

Dropping the peeler among the pile of peelings on the damp newspaper, she sat next to him at the kitchen table and looked into his eyes.

'What's happened?' she asked.

'I got a call at work today.'

'Yes,' she replied slowly.

'We're getting our baby girl. On Monday!'

'What? Monday? I don't have anything ready!'

'Well, we've got the weekend to get ready,' he reassured her with his lovable grin.

'Oh, Ian!' she cried, searching for her hanky under her bra strap. 'We've waited so long for our baby girl.'

'Yes, we have. And she'll be here on Monday.'

'Let's tell the boys,' she said.

They went into the lounge room where Neil and Jeff squirmed their gangly legs around the rug on the floor as they watched TV; they did not appreciate the interruption.

Neil could tell Mum had been crying and sat up to see what was wrong. Jeff turned the volume down and they sat in silence while they were told the news that was going to change everything around their home.

Mum took each of their hands in hers and said, 'Boys, you know that we've been waiting a long time to adopt a baby girl.'

Dad continued, 'Today I received a phone call at work with the news our baby girl will be delivered to us on Monday.'

Relieved it was happy news, my brothers paused momentarily before bombarding Mum and Dad with questions. Mum lovingly responding with reassuring hugs and kisses.

In a tailspin of excitement and panic, Mum suddenly felt completely unprepared. There was nothing in the house for a baby! No cot, nappies, bottles, clothes – nothing! They were leaving the next day to visit family in Muswellbrook, so Mum spent the weekend with her sister-in-law gathering as much as possible.

I struggle to imagine the enormity of the situation; in a time without easy access to telephones, cars and shops, and while looking after two young boys, the flurry of organisation was no mean feat. At some point, Mum contacted a dear friend, Maureen, who had two young boys and a car. In the 1960s, having (or receiving) babies was deemed women's business. Dad had to be at work on Monday, leaving Mum in need of Maureen's help to pick me up. This and that and a whole lot more was arranged over the weekend, amidst the trip to Muswellbrook. Whatever the upheaval was for Mum and Dad, the news and waves of activity that surrounded my brothers was some indication their lives were about to change, like the rest of us.

I was born at Crown Street Women's Hospital in Sydney. My adoption was deferred due to a medical condition which meant my legs required plastering. I've often wondered about that first month of my life. Even as I write this, my heart aches, my throat tightens and my eyes blur with tears. Since becoming a mother myself, I've come to understand and appreciate the early days and weeks in the life of a newborn, and their primal need for physical contact. I know nothing of my environment in those early days, but I assume I was still at the hospital, kept in a crib with regimented feeding, changing, bathing and sleeping times. Presumably there were moments when I was held close and cuddled by the nurses, maybe a kiss on my forehead, or my little fingers curled around the finger of someone who held me. I'll never know. But I hope. Nobody can recall the first month of my life for me, and that's just that.

Things were soon to change.

Newly arrived baby Karen with big brothers Jeffrey and Neil

SPECIAL DELIVERY – 8 MARCH 1965

Many of the tellings of my story have led to imaginings of the un-named characters, of people I would never know. I've often thought about my journey from the hospital in Sydney into the arms of my parents in Newcastle, and especially about the nurse who got me there. What was it like for her?

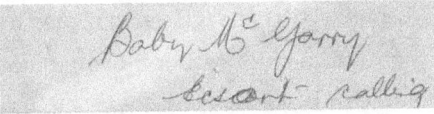

The name tag tied to my wrist by the nurse who left me at the station

∞

LIKE ANY OTHER DAY, I arrived at work ten minutes before my shift started in the maternity ward at Crown Street Women's Hospital. Living with my parents and little brother in Sydney's outer suburbs meant my two connecting buses had me arriving at Surry Hills at a quarter to the hour, any hour. It was just as well; I hated being late and rushed for anything, especially for Matron. I would do anything to avoid her wrath.

Carefully following the instructions in the papers waiting for me at the desk, I collected the precious bundle into my arms, along with a satchel containing nappies, bottles, wraps and paperwork. The enormous weight and responsibility strained my arms, my shoulders and a piece of my heart. From the moment I walked down the stairs of Crown Street and during the taxi ride to Central Station I focused on nothing but my instructions and the scheduled timing of departure on the Newcastle Flyer. It was a relief to be sitting on the moving train, bound for the destination where the precious cargo I was holding would be handed over.

The cityscape made way for suburban backyards and the rooftops of Sydney flickered by. It wasn't until I saw the bushland of Ku-ring-ai Chase National Park, and eventually the bridge over the mystical Hawkesbury River, that it dawned on me what a journey this baby was on. It was her new beginning. I looked at her little head and tiny hands and considered what might lie ahead. I'm not sure where she came from or really where she was going, apart from the arms of her new and hopefully loving family in Newcastle. Who would she become? What would open up before her?

In 1965 the Church of England arranged many adoptions, so I was certain the baby in my arms would be handed over to a good Christian family, all in the best interests of the child. Whoever had been the woman to carry and deliver this baby, most likely an unmarried woman who had found her way to trouble, she was not this baby's mother, and she would do well to forget all about having had a baby at all. As I considered the future of this innocent child, I whispered a little prayer over her head, praying for God to look after her, and that she would find love, care and kindness.

It was a fleeting moment of prayer, which didn't come as naturally to me as it did to the other women in my family. I was more pragmatic and interested in doing a job well, seeing it through, being punctual and keeping out of trouble with Matron. Keeping an eye on my watch, I managed to avoid the gaze of the other passengers. My uniform told anyone who saw me of my occupation, and the fact I was holding an infant in my arms further illustrated I was on hospital business. Adoption wasn't unusual, however it was rarely spoken about in polite company. When it was mentioned, it was in hushed tones, laden with judgement 'in the interest of the child'.

The train was due at Broadmeadow station at 11.45am, where I was to hand over the baby to her adoptive mother. My instructions clearly stated I had fifteen minutes for this transaction before I had to board the same train again, on its journey back to Sydney. Missing this return journey was not an option and in Matron's eyes would be the equivalent of abandoning my post, going AWOL.

Disembarking carefully from the carriage, holding the newborn and the satchel, I noticed about a dozen people on the platform, some reuniting with passengers, others hurriedly going about their business, some wayward stragglers. I looked around for the woman to whom I was to hand over the infant. Nobody came forth. I organised myself on the wooden seat abutting the platform signage that said 'Broadmeadow', carefully checking my instructions and the time on my watch. I checked it against the platform clock. My watch and the clock were a few minutes out, which made me nervous.

The station master approached, patrolling the platform after the train left. It would complete the remaining two stops to Newcastle before commencing its return trip to Sydney. He confirmed my travel arrangements, and understood the need for me to be on the train as it arrived back at the opposite platform in the next ten minutes or so. I wasn't sure which minute hand I could place my trust in. He invited me into his office and offered to take charge of the baby and her satchel, with some confidence that the recipient would arrive soon.

Feeling increasingly anxious that my return passage to Sydney would be arriving imminently, I accepted his offer. With a moment to spare I fashioned a tag which I fastened, using a ribbon from the dummy, around the baby's wrist. 'Baby McGarry – Escort calling.' It was my best hope that this precious parcel would be collected by the right person. I hurriedly thanked the station master; handing him the baby, I barely had a moment to look down at her. I raced up the platform, up forty wooden stairs, across the bridge that took me to another forty stairs, descending to the platform opposite. Breathless, I ran faster. I could hear the distant sound of the approaching train becoming louder. I stood facing the platform where I'd left the baby with her tag on her wrist, and her satchel. The Sydney Flyer arrived. I had two and a half hours to consider the anonymous people in whose lives and new beginnings I'd played a part.

SPECIAL DELIVERY – 8 MARCH 1965

∞

THERE HAS ALWAYS BEEN a minor point of contention in the telling of this story. Was the train early? Or were Mum and Maureen running late? Whatever the truth, there was nobody at the station to collect me when the nurse got off the train. I would never have fully believed this fairy tale so many years later, but Mum showed me the small cardboard tag the nurse had made for my wrist showing my original family name. I've continued to wonder about the nurse with whom I spent more than three hours, the woman who made that decision to leave me with the station master. I've thought about that man who was in receipt of a baby, labelled like any other parcel, awaiting collection. What did they say to me? How did they respond to me? Did they ever wonder about me again?

PRECIOUS PETALS

Feeling special and lucky became ingrained into my psyche from a young age. It had the potential to make me precocious, yet I was amazed by my own story. It gave me a reason to wonder about the cast and characters, known and unknown, in my own story; a story outline, waiting for colour and shade to bring it to life. Mum affirmed my belonging in the most unlikely of situations. On Saturday mornings, shopping down the street always involved going to the paper shop and bumping into people I didn't know, usually an older lady or gent from church who appeared to know all about me.

'Oh!' they'd exclaim. 'Is this…?'

'Yes!' Mum would beam back.

'Oh isn't she beautiful, what a lovely smile,' would be a common response.

'She certainly is our special girl,' Mum would often reply, or words to that effect.

On several of many trips to DJs (David Jones) in town, I experienced a similar scenario. I remember waiting in line with bright eyes to be served by the polished female sales assistants. The impeccable black-and-white uniform set off manicured nails, coifed hairstyle, sheer stockings and black, patent-leather shoes. I was mesmerised. I never minded the wait. I'd watch the ladies intently as they served customers, treating them like they were the only people in the store. Folding the garments carefully, sometimes using tissue paper to separate the body from the sleeves, and tearing black-and-white patterned wrapping paper from the huge roll with the sharpest blade. The sound of that tear tore through me with glee, it really did. The perfect fold in the paper – over, together, down, up – followed by the rhythmic sound of the sticky tape dispenser – pulling, stretching, cutting – and the precise placement of the tape on the paper. So much care and pride shown with each wrapping – it's surprising I observed any of the accompanying chit-chat while being so entranced. Maybe it was my avid interest in what the sales assistant was doing that caused them to notice me, or maybe it was their professionalism – they would always comment on how I looked. Often Mum would pipe up with a comment that would draw me into the banter.

'Yes, this is my daughter,' she'd say as she looked lovingly down on me with immense pride, her beautiful blue eyes sparkling, her smile beaming.

'She's very special, we waited a long time for her. We chose her, you see.'

And I did feel special. Mum had so many ways to make me feel so wanted. I felt special and treasured, like a precious gift. 'Precious' and 'Petals' were her pet names for me and they have always filled my being with love, pride and thankfulness. Many people of the time were familiar with adoption, or at least had heard stories about someone they knew who was adopted and it wasn't unusual that store attendants were generous and interested. I imagine now it was because adoption was more widely known and understood, but at the time it felt like I was the centre of the universe. Mum was very good at giving out some information without telling the whole story. The fact she and I knew what she was talking about seemed to be the main point; whether or not the sales assistants gathered fully what was going on, I'll never know – they were of course very professional. Mum and I always walked away holding hands or linking arms and again I felt my existence was affirmed and so very welcome.

Despite being utterly wanted and adored, the weight of expectation that came with being the long-awaited baby girl was enormous. I mostly lapped up the love and guidance from my family and my church, but by the time I was a child of the seventies, I had become aware that a bigger life was waiting for me out there. I often started sentences with 'I can't wait…' Mum and Dad often encouraged me to slow down and 'not grow up too fast.' Being a good girl was paramount, making good impressions on others, being polite and seen to do the right thing, by teachers, neighbours, friends and strangers; this was reinforced through my extra-curricular activities, of which I had many. I managed a busy schedule, which through primary school was fairly rare for my peers. I guessed it was because I was 'special' and being groomed to be a nice young lady who would get a good job after school until I married a nice young man and had a lovely life raising my own children. That was the expectation.

ANSWERS AND QUESTIONS

I grew up with fairly fuss-free food, which also meant very little international culinary influences. Meat and three veg was the staple tea six days out of seven, with alternating 'takeaway' nights presenting either a barbeque chook or fish and chips. Home-delivery didn't exist and only very occasionally did we go out for Chinese specialising in 'Australian' food, which mostly meant omelettes and peas. Our local fish 'n' chipper was run by Tony and Maria, the only people of ethnic origin I'd ever known. Cardiff in Newcastle was a particularly white-bread place, without a hint of wholemeal, let alone multi-grain. Tony and Maria made an impression as I intently observed them many times waiting for our family order to be cooked. Both had shiny olive skin and a few gold teeth between them, Maria's hair was the frizziest I'd seen, and Tony's the greasiest. I wondered if their complexion was due to the lack of sunlight and exposure to fresh air, because they always seemed to be working and sweating over the deep fryer.

I was largely left to my own devices over the long summer holidays, even if in the company of Mum. Boredom gave me countless hours to dream, imagine, role-play and wonder. Without fail some of the fun was interrupted by sorting out the linen and tupperware cupboards. One day of these summer days, when I was eight years old, I had the contents of the linen press surrounding me on the hallway floorboards, when Mum gave me some information that would forever change the way I saw myself.

'Do you know why we chose Ann as your middle name?' she asked.

I had no idea as there were no other Anns I knew of in the family.

'Ann is the name of your birth mother.'

'How do you know?' I questioned, momentarily thinking Mum might have met her. 'We were sent a little information about her when you arrived.'

Somehow it helped me feel connected to my birth mother. I'd spent a long while imagining meeting her, one day. I'd often dreamed and day-dreamed and romanticised about who she was, what she'd look and be like as a person. I wondered if she could've been the lady from the milk-bar across the road from my school, from whom I regularly bought 5-cents-worth of mixed lollies in a white paper bag. What if it was her! I wondered if she knew I was her daughter, if she recognised me. I spent a lot of time wondering if I would recognise my birth mother if I ever saw her, or if I would feel something twinge inside of me. What if I already had seen her or met her, without knowing? I felt sure I didn't know her and anyway, I was born in Sydney and lived in Newcastle, a long way from where my birth mother would be. Dreaming, musing and imagining I could be anyone in the world always comforted me. Far-flung thoughts that I could be the daughter of someone famous, or maybe a princess in a castle, were a convenient outlet for my imagination, and gave me a real sense of possibility and potential. I knew one day I'd discover my truth, but for now I was happy to dream up the possibilities.

The other thing Mum told me that day as I cleaned out the linen press was some information about my father. Now I'm not sure if I really knew about the facts of life at that stage. I was eight years old and brought up in a fairly conservative environment. My brother was married that year, so coupling up was definitely within my sphere of knowledge, and the broad understanding that after couples get married they have babies. I don't think I'd given much thought to my biological father up until this point, all the previous focus had been on my 'real mum,' who couldn't keep me. Mum telling me I had a father was a bit of a shock, but I was also excited. Here's someone else I could include in my daydreams, like another character in a fantastic story. Then Mum dropped the biggest bombshell of my short life.

'I also have some interesting information about your biological father.'

'Really? What is it?' Thinking it would be a name or a clue to him being a famous actor. I sat on the floorboards in the hallway, looking up at Mum perched on a stool, my eager eyes wide and my little mind open, ready for what was next.

'Well, he is Italian.'

Italian? I was horrified! This was the worst news ever. I let out a little cry as I crumbled and cried on the inside. All I could think was it meant I would grow up to look like Maria from the fish 'n' chip shop! I didn't want frizzy hair, or gold teeth or shiny olive skin! I was eight years old and Maria and Tony were the only people I knew in the whole world who were Italian. (Forty years later I learned Tony and Maria were actually Greek).

As is often the way, people generally want to recognise themselves in their kin, or to see themselves in others. From the moment a child is born there is a preoccupation that they look like someone in the family, living or passed. Photos are compared and competitive claims made, which continue throughout the developmental phases of a young person's life. I was first told I looked like someone when I was ten years old, dancing with my brother Jeff, at Neil's wedding. I was so excited and proud to be ballroom dancing with my big brother, completely unaware that people were watching us. When the photos came back after the wedding there was a great photo of us dancing, both of our eyes facing downward, in the moment, both of us with dark shiny wavy hair. That's when I heard people exclaim how much we looked alike. It was a pivotal moment for me, the proclamation about us looking alike emphasising the fact that I really had never looked like anyone before. People needed me to fit into the family mould. I didn't know at the time, but I needed it, too.

That was the first, and last, time familial comparisons were made about my physical appearance in the Forbes family. Family mannerisms, however, were being efficiently and effectively absorbed. Like all young people I was a sponge, a really spongy sponge. I was also an extrovert. I played to a crowd, milked an

Dancing with Jeff, at Neil's wedding 1975

audience and relished any chance I had to perform. Neil gave me a t-shirt that said 'Acting the goat', which everyone thought was hilarious and I wore with pride. I was drawn to a camera like a moth to a flame, and when no camera was in sight my imagination was large enough to contain an Opera House-sized audience, whether in my backyard applauding my physical stunts on the verandah balustrades and swing set, on the front verandah bouncing my ball, in my bedroom performing piano concertos, recording mock-radio programs and news broadcasts, singing in front of a mirror into my hairbrush, or into a shampoo bottle in the bath. At this stage of my life, Jeff and Neil had both married and moved out of home. I was still in primary school and living a life which largely resembled that of an only child. A girl like me had to amuse herself and fortunately I found myself highly amusing.

GROWING UP YOUNG

Over time my identity evolved from being 'chosen' to being 'adopted'. 'I'm adopted,' I'd say whenever it came up. Throughout primary school it was either uncommon or just never really discussed by other people. Often my statement was met with whispers and darting glances or people didn't know how to respond. This was still a time when adoption was common, and adoption within families would also have been prevalent. I was born just prior to the introduction of the contraceptive pill; certainly before single mothers were socially accepted or a legal entity. I was blissfully unaware at the time of the judgement and speculation about the unfortunate situation my biological mother must have 'gotten herself into' to have a baby, and the assumption she was probably a teenager when she 'got into trouble.' I anticipated my 'real mum' – an awful term that I sometimes used, only occasionally correcting others who used it – would have been a lot younger than my 'mum-mum.' I drew this conclusion due to the fact I had much older brothers. Mum was the grand age of thirty-two when I arrived, considered rather old for the time, and by the time she was forty-two she was a grandmother. By today's standards, my assumptions and occasional embarrassment at the age of my mum is absurd, but at the time, truth be told, Mum was much older than the mothers of my friends. It wasn't just age, sometimes it seemed there was a generation between my parents and my friends' parents. One mum in particular blew my mind with her glamour and edginess. I was in Year 5 and she picked up her daughter, my best friend, Trudy from school. I'll never forget how she looked. Margo was everything my mum wasn't. Tight denim jeans, platform shoes, black afro-styled hair, huge sunnies, a stunning cleavage and long fingernails painted in black-and-white stripes; this was 1975 and she was 1975 like I'd never seen. I'd been living in a parallel universe, just around the corner, which became even more pronounced on a visit to their house – a two-storey, Spanish-mission-style house with a spiral staircase. A group of us hung out there after school one day with no adults present, as both Trudy's parents were working. One thing led to another and I copped my first eyeful of pornography, found under the mattress of my best friend's mum and dad. It was horrifying! Happy to be home that night, safely cocooned from the wide world, I felt good about the fact my mum was older and a lot more conservative than Margo. I wasn't ready for that.

The newly arrived Scottish neighbours next door brought some much-needed relief and distraction to my solitary existence. They fitted out their garage like a rumpus room, which was a great place to hang out, when invited. The other Scottish neighbours, two doors up, had an above-ground pool. All around the new housing estate where we lived, blocks of land were being cleared and houses were in various states of construction. It was quite the playground; possessing a wild imagination and without much supervision, I had a ball. The biggest hazard in our neighbourhood was the occasional dog who roamed free, without any known obligation from owners to keep cranky dogs secured behind fences.

I became firm friends with the boy next door. His name was Andrew, and he had blonde hair, blue eyes, light freckles and a fantastic Scottish accent. His dad drove an orange Charger, *the* definitive car of the 70s. He also wore flares, purple shirts, jewellery and had huge sideburns. He was the grooviest looking dad I'd ever seen. Andrew had an older sister and his mum was pregnant. Time spent in their garage with the neighbourhood kids was lots of fun. We played spin the bottle and, at eleven years of age, things were thankfully innocent and mostly hilarious.

I started to really, really like Andrew, who was also a high school boy. Valentine's Day was approaching, and I felt compelled to write my first ever love letter 'from your secret admirer.' Before placing it in his letterbox I wanted to run it by a couple of my friends at school. Dad dropped me off at Gillian's place on his way to work, as usual, and we walked to school from there. I loved those mornings. Like clockwork, Mrs Mitchell would be standing at the kitchen sink in her dressing gown, combing Gillian's part with a wet comb, tying her long plaits with yellow ribbons. Some days I'd get a peek into her teenage brother's bedroom from the hallway, where I first caught a glimpse of a leather-clad Suzie Quatro poster on his wall, a wink to an enticing future of possibilities. I made sure I had the love letter in the pocket of my uniform as I got into the car, but when I arrived at Gillian's I couldn't find it anywhere. At first I was disappointed, then became annoyed because I really wanted her advice on what I'd written.

After a long and eventful day in Year 6, I began the long and winding walk home. My school port was heavy and I was tired. I said goodbye to most of my friends on the main road, and turned off onto the winding bush track towards home. My hands were blistered from swapping my port from one to the other. So sick of my heavy load and wishing hard I didn't have to carry it all the way home, I thought of a solution. Opening it up, I pulled out my orange plastic skipping rope and tied one end to the port's handle and the other end around my waist. I proceeded to drag it behind me up the winding track. It made a helluva noise, which I was sure would be good for deterring snakes and lizards as well. Feeling pretty pleased with myself, I didn't anticipate what would happen next. When I arrived home, Mum was furious. Dragging my port behind me up the dirt track had scraped the daylights out of its surface. It looked really bad and I was in big trouble.

It got worse. I was in even bigger trouble for something else. Mum came towards me in the hallway, waving my love letter to Andrew in her hand. I couldn't believe my eyes.

'What do you think this is, young lady?' she spat at me.
I choked on my gasping breath. The letter! I ran to my room and dived onto my bed with extreme embarrassment. After a

quiet dinner I couldn't wait to go to my room. I could hear Mum and Dad engrossed in whispered tones over the dining table. They called me back out...

'Karen Ann, we are *very* disappointed in you. It seems that we have a problem. This letter shows us that you are clearly *boy crazy*!' These words rang in my ears for years to come...

'That's why, next year we'll be sending you to Newcastle Church of England Girls' Grammar School!'

I was shattered! 'No, No, No, *no*, I won't!'

'Yes you will, young lady,' came the retort.

'If I go there, I'll become a *lesbian*!' I ran as fast as I could into my room, diving on my bed, this time in despair.

The look on my mother's face was funny and scary at once. I'm not sure if she'd ever heard the word before, but if she had, she certainly didn't expect me to know it. Luckily, I had the rest of the year to get used to the idea of leaving every single friend behind. They were off to the local public high school, the same one my brothers had been to, but I was off to a *girls'* school in town. If I wasn't boy crazy before I went there, I sure as hell was by the time I left.

IMAGINING GRANDEUR

Dreaming and fantasising about my heritage has been constant throughout my life, ebbing and flowing, but always there like an escape valve, providing comfort when I felt out of place. Similar to my daydreams of being an actress, on stage or film, or even on a street corner, I gravitated to the places of my imagination, where the impossible was possible, where stories came to life and where I could try out endless versions of being. For the longest time it felt like my destiny. I desperately wanted to be in a play, to memorise lines of a script, to embody a character and perform. Little tastes and teasers throughout primary school were wonderful, but never enough.

Every fibre of my being filled my performance as a green bean in the primary school production of Jack and the Beanstalk. I was as stellar as any green bean could've 'bean'. Another unforgettable performance on a local stage had me singing. 'My legs are kind of bowed from all the horses that I've rode, through the salt-bush and the sand, I've got the rock 'n' rollin' beat from the rollin' saddle seat, from living in the never-never land', while wearing a caramel suede A-line skirt with matching vest, trimmed with cream fringe and teamed with a sky-blue blouse.

A more serious and powerful performance, so I was told, was at a Girl Guide presentation of a Dreamtime creation story. I was cast as the sun. My costume had me wearing black for the first time, leotard and stockings, upon my head an enormous papier-mâché head-dress of sun rays. My entrance was slow and measured, my silent gestures cued by the narration. That performance brought rave reviews, which surprised me – it all came so naturally. I felt connected to the part without really trying. I was in the zone without speaking or acting the goat. I loved the ceremonial aspects of performance.

Ritual and ceremony were present throughout my childhood at weekly church services. I wanted to be part of it, but the role of 'server' was deemed inappropriate for girls. The wearing of robes, lighting of candles, forming part of the procession, carrying and placing the chalice and associated cloths relating to communion, and the reading of lessons remained firmly out of my reach.

I was, however, allowed to look after the children in Sunday school, a role deemed more appropriate for a young lady. Later I joined the junior choir. At least I got to sing, although it was rarely comfortable. The keys were firmly entrenched – no variations would ever be made. Singing in the church choir was another instance of not fitting the mould, which at the time I thought a problem.

Elvis Presley had been my idol ever since I can remember – my love was spawned by movies and weekend TV matinees. For an isolated, boy-crazy, only child, this was the highlight of my life! My first record bought with my own money was the soundtrack to *Roustabout* featuring great songs like 'Little Egypt'. Oh, the posters, the dreams I had. ABBA had also started to dominate my musical diet. Their video clips on *Countdown* blew my mind. I remember exactly where I was when I first heard them. Back in Year 4, at a forgotten person's birthday party in a garage in Belmont. 'Rock Me' rocked me to my tiny core. I was totally hooked. A year or so later, ABBA toured Australia, and dates were set in Sydney. How could I possibly get to the ABBA concert? I lived in suburban Newcastle, a three-hour drive from Sydney, and my family had zero interest or willingness to indulge my 'passing phase' of needing to attend a concert in Sydney.

I didn't want to go to an ABBA concert with my parents anyway, even if they had agreed to take me, so I needed to find some people who would. I proposed to Mum and Dad that I could organise a bus from Cardiff if I did some door-knocking in the neighbourhood to see who else would be interested. I'd need about thirty people and I worked out the cost of the tickets and a bus. I might have been only ten years old, but I felt confident this was within my scope. Apart from the two families in my street I hung out with, the steep hill didn't encourage community connection. Nevertheless, off I trundled from door to door with the opening line, 'Hi, I'm Karen from number 21 and I'm trying to get together a bus of people to go to the ABBA concert in Sydney. Is there anyone here who would be interested?'

It's fair to say the response was mixed, but thankfully nobody slammed the door in my face. I'm sure there were some bemused reactions as well as mild interest, but absolutely nowhere near the numbers I needed to make it viable. My parents were no use at all, and I think they let me do it all myself knowing full well it wouldn't work, and that would be the end of that. And it was. I never made it to see ABBA. The following Christmas I was given some ABBA knee-high socks – a pathetic consolation. I continued hanging on to ABBA lyrics, tapes and film clips whenever I could.

Another time I took it upon myself to show some entrepreneurship was more spontaneous. One day after arriving home from school I noticed a glossy magazine in our letterbox.

Quick as a flash I grabbed it and realised it was a quality shopping catalogue. I hadn't seen anything like it before. This was many years before 'junk mail', and I saw considerable value in such a catalogue. Without hesitation I took it upon myself to follow through with a most brilliant money-making plan. Mum was busying herself getting tea ready when I left the house, still wearing my school uniform. It was about five in the afternoon as I walked up and down my steep street, collecting a catalogue from each letterbox. Stone-faced and with complete confidence, if not entitlement, I knocked on every front door and offered to sell them catalogues for 5 cents. Everyone who was home, and some who were just pulling into their driveways after work, bought the catalogue. It was so easy! Feeling incredibly accomplished, I walked through my front door and headed for my bedroom. The rattling change in my uniform pocket caught Mum's attention.

'What's that noise?' she asked.

'Nothing,' I replied.

'Karen Ann – where have you been?'

Within minutes she asked enough questions to elicit a confession. I wasn't ashamed, I was actually quite proud, but I knew she wouldn't feel the same. She really roused on me and I got into *big* trouble. There were many tears before the consequence was delivered.

'Well, young lady, you will be going back to every house and tell every person what you have done. You will then return their 5 cents, with an apology!'

I was furious and disappointed my ingenuity was not celebrated. No way was I able to do that! It would be the most embarrassing thing in the world.

'You either do it yourself, or I will come with you to each and every door!' She shouted down my resistance.

Her threat was enough to get me moving. Mum walked with me and waited on the footpath to make sure I returned the money. Most of the people smiled at me or thanked me, some laughed and some refused to take the refund – but Mum made sure I insisted. It had been a character-building and great idea, albeit a little misguided, and really didn't get the credit it deserved.

My new, all-girls high school didn't lend itself much to theatre studies. In my first year there was a fantastic production of *Oliver!* but it was decided that my first school production would be our last – apparently it took too much time away from class, causing a distraction from regular studies. Good one. It was 1979 and I was in Year 9, and this was the year I managed to orchestrate another idea, this time to greater effect.

Desperate to put on a show, I convinced my friends and classmates we could put on a lunchtime concert for charity; a musical tribute to the decades of rock 'n' roll through costume and dance, supported by a narrator (me). With the backing of my friends I approached a teacher, who pitched it to someone with a little more sway – probably the assistant principal. The idea got through, so planning and production could gather steam. And it did.

With some group consultation the songs were nominated and a final selection was made, informed by accessibility to material and its cultural relevance. Basically, I tried to get Elvis, The Beatles and some Aussie rock on the bill. I admitted defeat with Elvis as 'Jailhouse Rock' didn't have the mass-appeal we needed. My Elvis impersonations, spontaneously unleashed at various parties, already provided a much-needed personal creative outlet, so I moved on. 'Rock Around the Clock' made the final cut to represent the 50s, The Beatles version of 'Twist and Shout' for the 60s and The Angels' 'Shadow Boxer' represented the current decade. Three groups self-nominated to perform a mime and/or dance with costumes to match. I wrote the script for my narration, introducing each decade of music and performance.

Sourcing the songs was problematic. I waited for Sunday night's request show on the local radio, and called in several weeks in a row, waiting for my call to be answered and my request for the older songs granted. My fingers had to be at the ready to press play and record on my radio-cassette player to capture the three songs. The production values were minimal to none.

With a ten-cent entry fee, the whole school community, around 250 students, attended the one-off lunchtime concert. We raised a grand $25 for the starving children of Kampuchea – an important and popular global cause at the time, which drew much attention thanks to a horrendous and effective TV campaign. Whether or not our performance was received critical acclaim I can't be sure – it wasn't really the point. We had a ball.

BELONGING

I always felt included and part of the family, even when there was an undeniable and recurring feeling of being an outsider. My brothers had full and productive lives of their own; in fact, I don't ever remember a time when they didn't. They belonged to their soccer clubs, their long-term girlfriends became their wives, and they were connected to our cousins in a way I was not – mainly due to our age differences. They'd come over for mid-week dinners, and we'd have a chance to sit around after the meal in the lounge room with the tele on in the background until it was my bedtime and I had to leave the room full of conversation and company. I hated it yet I complied, but not without attitude. Occasionally I'd hang in the hallway listening to their babble – the veneered louvre doors separating our worlds. I retreated into my room, my safe space where my dreams could give me the freedom and belonging I desired.

Of course, I was different to everyone in my family. Somewhere out there I had another story. I knew it would come to me at some stage and I really didn't want to rush it. The time I had, the time I needed inside my head to explore the unknown, the possibilities of who I might become, who

I'd been, where I came from, was endless. I needed to be alone with this dreaming.

Faith was integral to my being. I had always known love and I'd always yearned for story. Stories from my ancestors. My curiosity was satiated by long and drawn-out moments spent with my dad's parents, Mumma and Poppa, as I lay on the daybed in their kitchen asking endless questions while they went about their chores.

'What was your mother's name?'
'Who were your brothers and sisters?'
'What did they do?'
'What were you like as a little girl?'
'What games did you play?'
'When did you meet each other?'
'What was Dad like as a little boy?'
'Tell me about the olden days.'

As I began each conversation, I got the feeling the olden days didn't seem as interesting to the old people as they were to me. I was fascinated by the people who went before me, the lives they led, the decisions they made, all that influenced the lives of their children, and their children's children, which included me.

Sitting on the back step of Mumma and Poppa's, I could see through the wire fence to the house at the back, the house I arrived at when I was a four-week-old baby. We moved to the other side of the railway line when I was about a year old, the home where my first memories were made. A wooden pedestrian bridge crossed the tracks between our place and Mumma and Poppa's and the Cardiff shops. We were still a one-car family and we didn't have a phone.

I have always been comforted by the sound of trains in the medium distance, which must have some basis in those early years living in the shadow of the railway line. Occasionally Dad needed to get up very early to catch the Flyer to Sydney. He'd get on at Broadmeadow station, and by the time it passed our back door I'd be there with Mum waiting to wave a tea towel at him. He'd always try and get a window seat, and he'd watch for us, and we'd see him wave his newspaper in the window in reply. I thought that was the best thing ever.

Every Sunday began with Sunday school and church. These days were busy and full of many social occasions, like picnics and dances and raising money through fetes and raffles and dinners. They were communal and social times. There were not a lot of kids my age hanging around these events, so the ones that did gravitated toward each other. I always felt welcome, but I didn't really belong. I was marking time, waiting for something to happen.

I loved going to school in the city, I loved the independence it gave me even as it governed my presentation to the world. The uniform code was strict, and we were the only students in the whole of Newcastle who had to wear hats. One of the many rules was that we were forbidden to eat while walking, or sitting at bus stops or train stations. Our school was perched on top of Newcastle Hill, opposite Newcastle Cathedral, our school chapel. I've always felt an overwhelming sense of calm whenever I've been inside that cathedral. It connected me with my family's faith, my school's values and my friends, and maybe something more, a feeling I couldn't quite pin down. Wednesday mornings began with chapel. Every student from the school would cross the road and enter the cathedral. There'd be prayers, a lesson from the bible, and it would end with the school song – 'To be a Pilgrim'. The sound of singing voices in that cathedral made my heart soar. There was so much about that whole precinct that has been etched into my psyche. The school itself was a hotchpotch of old buildings with a few new ones. The art room was perched even higher on a hill at the rear of the land, and from its doorstep the view of terracotta rooftops, the cathedral, treetops, the Obelisk, hills and seagulls with the whiff of ocean breeze was incredible and not lost on a self-absorbed teenage girl.

The needlework room upstairs from the principal's office overlooked the Watt Street Mental Hospital. Beyond its walls, a row of buildings and a sliver of oceanic horizon beckoned. A bay window had two sewing machines in front of it, the most coveted spot in the room. It was always a wonderful day when I secured this spot, and it was especially lucky when hang-gliders floated past. The view of these flying men with enormous wingspans, gliding before me, up, over, under and beyond toward the horizon took my mind with them. The freedom of flight juxtaposed with the entrapment of the patients below in Watt Street is an image I've never forgotten. The walled quadrangle of Watt Street provided the only open-air space for the patients, who slowly paced around in what I imagine to be a drug-induced stupor to dull their mental torment. Occasionally we would have sport within those walls, usually playing softball or jogging, in full view of the patients who were both physically and mentally bound. There were times when one of the patients would escape and be found wandering the surrounding streets and, on rare occasions, within the school grounds.

The walk down the hill every afternoon from school to catch the bus or train home took me past Watt Street, past the Newcastle Court House, the Grand Hotel (where in a matter of years I would become a regular), down Bolton Street, past the Newcastle Herald building and toward Newcastle Station on Scott Street. If I was catching the 363 or the 365 bus to Cardiff, I'd turn right into Hunter Street at the point of the majestic marker of the Newcastle Post Office. Hungry John's, the greasy takeaway, was diagonally opposite this grand architectural icon. Further east up Hunter Street was Royal Newcastle Hospital and the nurse's accommodation, both of which sat on prime real estate, across the road from Newcastle beach. Hungry John's did great business, being smack-bang at one of the first bus stops for all routes departing Hunter Street. Because school rules forbade us from being seen eating in the street in school uniform, we managed to cheat the system by ordering our (potato) scallops – two for 5 cents, while standing across the doorway. Our feet were technically not on the street, but we could look out for our buses.

One summer weekday afternoon I opted for a chocolate paddle-pop instead of the scallops. Leaning on the wall of the shop, in the doorway, I unwrapped it to feel the icy chocolate cream on my tongue. Girls on the street in front of me, not eating, started to chatter loudly and point up the street. I looked up and to the right and saw a magnificent looking woman dressed in black and white, wearing large sunglasses and a wide-brimmed hat, holding the arm of a middle-aged man with thinning reddish-brown hair and pocked skin. He was also wearing sunglasses.

'Look who it is!' screamed someone.
I looked at him with disinterest. The reaction of the other girls was near hysterical. I stood my ground. Barely flinched. Kept my cool. I was still leaning against the wall, with my feet at the edge of the doorway. The couple walked towards us. The man let go of his female companion and came toward me and he said in a creepy voice, 'Can I have a lick of your ice-cream?'

To which I replied, 'No.'
He pulled back and walked on, ignoring everyone else in his path. He was Johnny O'Keefe.

File under 'Creeps I've met'.

Newcastle is a small city, and I enjoyed getting lost in the memories of those who went before me. One of my favourite stories Mum would tell was about Victory Day in 1945. She was thirteen years old and thousands of people gathered in Hunter Street to celebrate the end of World War II. That remains a moment in time that has always fascinated me: to experience the collective joy, elation and relief of knowing that the war had ended, but also the sorrow of the people who had suffered and died, and the loves they left behind. Mum described the party, the dancing in the street and the hugging of strangers and I would often reflect on this story as I walked around Hunter Street.

This whole area was my stomping ground. During the summer my friends and I would catch the train to Newcastle, walk up to Nobbys Beach or Newcastle Beach and hang out. I was never a fan of summer or the true beach culture, but I did a good job at faking it. I'd oil up and lie there on the baking sand, but I was always the first to crack. It was too friggin' hot! My school friends were much better suited to the beach lifestyle than me, they could lie still in the hot sun for much longer than I could. Although I'm compelled to have regular doses of coastal therapy, it doesn't involve hours sitting unprotected in the blaring sun.

In all of my dreaming, I'd imagined many scenarios. The day I'd get a tap on the shoulder while out shopping, or a series of phone calls where nobody would speak at the other end, just hang up after they heard my voice. Me, spying a beautiful woman with sad but kind eyes serving behind the counter, who I felt a sudden connection with, a woman I'd wait for across the road as she left work, watching how she walked, how she moved, her gestures, as if looking through a window into a world that could have been, but never was. Recognising familiarity in a woman in the news, in a magazine, on a screen – mostly it was me looking at her and making my way to her, with trepidation, as if I was about to intrude, to dredge, to interlope, interfere, without the intention of any of these things. I imagined a fearful first encounter, whenever it happened, with the ripple of emotion and hurt it could send to Mum and Dad, to her and her family. I was acutely aware of the impact my existence and appearance would have on my biological family members, and those close to them. For years these fears paralysed me in a dream state where I could imagine, where anything was possible, where the ending hadn't been written, a place where I could be a thousand variations of me. I could have been a welcomed treasure, a trigger for pain, a huge secret, one more, the only one, the long-lost one, the forgotten one. I loved to be alone in my dreaming. It was comforting and uncomfortable at the same time – a place I could soar and a place I could wallow. It was my place. The ending I wanted so badly would come in time, but how I loved living with the fantasy of possibilities.

The year I turned sixteen, 1981, was the first year after I left school I was and the year I had my first serious relationship. Remember, I was labelled 'boy crazy' at age eleven, and four years at a girls' school had done nothing to calm me down in that regard. My boyfriend, Tim, lived in Bar Beach and I lived in Macquarie Hills, a new housing estate developed in the 70s, on the fringe of Cardiff. Dad always maintained we still lived in Cardiff. Mum and I liked to call it Macquarie Hills. We were all right.

Tim had a couple of good friends who were going out with a couple of my friends. Ann-Maree was my best friend from 'Grammar', and we enjoyed many cosy, fun times in the convention of coupledom. Tim had an old Morris Minor that he spent much of his time meticulously renovating. I was a bit sad when he finally fixed the ignition after he'd spent over a year starting it with a wooden peg. I spent many hours of the weekend at his place in Wrightson Avenue, particularly on the driveway while he worked on his car, listening to his mixed tapes of alternative bands from Sydney and Brisbane, peppered with The Clash, The Cure, Sex Pistols, Blondie and The Ramones.

This was the beginning of a really influential time, I was exposed to more personal freedoms, which coincided with the exposure to all the bands Tim would play on his mixed tapes, including bootlegs of gigs he'd go to in Sydney. There were Australian bands that weren't yet considered mainstream, they blended surf and city sounds with attitudes of disaffection. The Sunnyboys, The Saints, The Riptides, The Reels, The Numbers, and XL Capris were home-grown east-coast bands whose bootlegs and bona-fide recordings made it onto our playlists. I was introduced to Monty Python and Cheech and Chong, and to the confounding talents of my male friends – who would memorise and recite lines, verse and interchanges verbatim, ad nauseam. Tim was in his final year at a Catholic boarding school in Sydney, which meant his net was cast wider than mine, and he was happy to take me along, for some of the ride. My brother Jeff and his wife Nina now had their third baby under five years and were living in Sydney, so there were extra reasons to visit my favourite city in the world.

My love affair with Sydney has been omnipresent throughout my whole life. The spectacular sight of the bridge, the harbour and the Opera House never fail to generate an electric buzz that extends to every nerve in my entire body. But it's more than that. Stories, songs and art set in Sydney provide me with a sense of belonging and an ownership that I have never really been able to articulate. XL Capris' song 'My City of Sydney' was, for a long time, my anthem. I took it with me when I eventually settled in Melbourne.

The fact that I was born in Sydney to an unknown woman was something that was completely mine and it separated me from my family. It was part of my unique identity and for a long time, that's all I had.

I was besotted with the water, the skyscrapers and the potential of a life well-lived with harbour views, a high-paying job and lots of friends who would journey with me. Until then, the occasional visits to my Sydney were with Mum and Dad, Mum and Dad and a school friend, later with Tim, and countless more with my lifelong friends and loves. I've partied hard in Sydney, loved, laughed, cried, danced, dined, worked, celebrated and had my heart broken. I've been inspired, comforted, confused, perplexed and angry in Sydney. For a woman who has never actually lived there, the city has shown me a lot.

At seventeen, I made the decision that when the time came to leave Newcastle – there was never any question that I would one day leave – I would not, could not, go to Sydney. Sydney would wait. If I was to live in Sydney it would be on my own terms, not just because it was the closest city to Newcastle. If I were ever to be able to live in Sydney, it would be when I could afford to live there. Sydney, Sydney, Sydney. I can talk, think, dream and feel it and never get sick of it.

GROWING UP A LADY

My time at Grammar was mostly good. There was much laughter and carrying-on with the girls. In many ways it was absolutely the right place for me to be – a small school. In other ways it wasn't – in no way did it prepare me for the big wide world; I was sheltered from it. My relationships with friends were close and intense, and all the while some of us had a strong sense we were marking time, like the marching parades I took part in while a school cadet. I loved the pomp and the ceremony; however, the meaning and purpose was non-existent. We were young ladies-in-waiting, until we were paired up with a suitable male in our late teens, and readied ourselves to become a wife of good standing and then to step into motherhood. Only a few of us imagined a career of any sort, or at least it was never imagined out loud. I dreamed of being an actor from a really young age, but it was never realised in my high school years. Mum and Dad made considerable sacrifices for me to attend Grammar, and at the same time Mum enjoyed me being at a private girls' school which was affiliated with the Newcastle Cathedral. She became involved in voluntary committees; in particular working in the book pool where she managed the recycling and re-purchasing of pre-loved textbooks. It was really good for her and she established some lasting friendships with some of the staff and parents.

As Year 10 approached there was no question it would be my final year at school. Newcastle was an industrial city with great beaches. Unemployment was high and it was written that I would be better off getting a trade and a job as soon as possible, which would set me up until I settled down and married. The only trades available to girls like me were typing, shorthand and bookkeeping. Back in Year 1, I was humiliated over maths sums and I became disengaged from anything relating to numbers, so bookkeeping would not be for me. So it was, at the end of Year 10 I left school at the age of fifteen to begin a TAFE course in secretarial studies. I was set. Or so I thought. In reality I was set up for a chain of jobs working for middle-aged, sexist, male power-mongers who took great advantage of my age, gender and cheerful demeanour. However, I will admit that to this day, touch-typing is one of the most important skills I've ever acquired.

My yearning for acting and drama studies hadn't waned, and as I'd left school at fifteen, Mum found a perfect way for me to be able to fulfil her ideal of me becoming a well-groomed young lady, while at the same time giving me the chance to study drama. There were no plays or productions at Anne Feneley's School of Speech and Deportment, instead there were plenty of poetry readings, recitals, monologues and exams. Miss Feneley herself (otherwise known as 'Madame') was the doyenne of Newcastle society. She taught deportment, modelling, speech and drama, and had a modelling agency.

A few talented students could straddle both catwalk and stage, fewer were hundred-per-centers; they could manage moving, speaking and smiling before the camera. I came in somewhere beneath the cream of the crop, but those heady days provided me with what I was led to believe were the essential ingredients – grace, diction and poise – to advance myself into a worthy participant in life, as a wife, and possibly, maybe even an actress. As Madame said to me on many occasions, in her husky and mature dulcet tones, 'Karen, darling, you know if you really want to be an actress, you must experience everything.'

Unbeknown to Madame, I *was* enjoying many experiences outside the inner sanctum of the self-important society rankings afforded to the few.

It was 1982 – I had bounced back from a broken heart after Tim and I broke up. I was seventeen, had my driver's licence and discovered punk rock. Nonetheless, I followed the doyenne's advice, at times reluctantly, at other times enthusiastically, and availed myself of many an experience. Only in retrospect did I query if the 'experiences' I was having equated to an unofficial internship, in which Madame received monetary and other benefits from patrons. At the time I thought her business model was more philanthropic. My parents trusted her and her reputation, and so did I. Her social standing was exceptional – how could we not be impressed? She hosted fashion parades for charity events and corporate sponsors, held in restaurants, halls, clubs, theatres and the local pub.

Madame pitched my first paid modelling gig as being in the Ladies Lounge of a pub in Wallsend one Saturday afternoon.

I would be modelling night wear.

'My parents wouldn't be happy for me to be modelling in a pub,' I told her.

She insisted. 'Oh no, Karen, dahling, it will be absolutely fine, I assure you – it won't be tacky. There'll be women attending as it will be held in the Ladies Lounge.'

She was very convincing. I'd been to many Tupperware parties with my mum, a few Sarah Coventry jewellery parties and Avon parties, so I knew that women liked getting together to look at products and buy things. The tried and true 'Karen, if you want to be an actress, you need to experience everything' line came out again. So I followed her advice.

Thankfully, my good friend Michelle came along with me for 'the experience,' even though she wasn't interested in becoming an actress. Arriving at the Lemon Grove Hotel in Wallsend it took only seconds to realise... this was Saturday afternoon at the pub after the local rugby game had finished. When I asked the bar staff to be shown to the Ladies Lounge, I was met with an indifferent stare.

'The catwalk will be here, they're just about to put it together,' the bartender told me.

'Here' was the public bar and 'the catwalk' was eight or so tables pushed together. Up three flights of old-school pub stairs was the dressing room, which is where I found the one other bemused model and a huge box of... *lingerie*.

We hurriedly worked out between us that while one of us was on the catwalk the other would be upstairs getting changed into the next outfit. Changes would need to be really quick because there were a lot of stairs between the change room and the catwalk. We picked out the pieces from the box. I went dibs on the long flowing items, the ones with sleeves – there weren't many of those. There were others at the bottom of the box. I pinched them between my thumb and forefinger, lifting them out of the box with a look of horror to show Michelle. Tiger-print patterned corsets, fishnets, garters – you get the drift. It wasn't that I didn't like that stuff, but I'd never worn any of it, let alone in front of a group of drunken men I'd never met. I was grateful that the other model offered to be first to hit the catwalk. Five minutes later I realised nothing could've prepared me for what I was cat-walking into.

The loud bunch of rugby-loving pissheads roared at the sight of nubile seventeen-year-old me in a silk nightgown, stepping up on a chair to reach the tables used to create a catwalk. The hungry men lined both sides of the catwalk, they were shouting out indecipherable sounds and then it started, in their own rhythmic timing akin to a hammer pounding steel, their fists thumped the tables – I mean, catwalk – as they chanted: 'Get it off! Get it off! Get it off!'

I let the gown slide off my shoulders, caught it on my right finger, slung it over my shoulder, wiggled my arse, then perfected my turn at the end of the catwalk, as I'd been taught. Cheers and hollers. Hollers and cheers. I finished that walk, stepped onto the chair, turned the corner and ran like mad. Not out of the pub like I desperately wanted. No. This was one of the 'experiences' I had to have, apparently. I ran as fast as I could, my heart pounding, up three flights of stairs. I passed the other model on her way down and arrived, panting, in front of Michelle, in the change room. She helped me with the next outfit as quickly as she could, and then… repeat. More cheers and hollers and more table thumping. I couldn't single any one man out of the crowd, they were a messy, murky, revolting mass of stale and stinky men, the like of whom I'd never seen before.

Walk, turn, walk, dismount, run like mad up three flights of stairs. Disrobe. Robe. Press-studs, hooks, eyes and ties. Check. Run downstairs, climb chair to tables, walk, turn, walk… repeat. This went on for what felt like an eternity. Then finally it came. The tiger-print corset. It was the finale. I put it on. I strutted my stuff. I did it. I just wanted it over with. That last struggle up the steps brought me, panting with exhaustion, to the change room where the three of us just looked at each other in amazement, like we'd just witnessed a freak accident.

We put the lingerie back in the box, got changed back into ourselves. For that experience I was to be paid $70, which I'd thought to be a large sum of hard-earned money. On Monday I received a phone call from Madame to say there had been a problem with the parade on Saturday and that I'd only be paid $35 because the owner of the lingerie shop wasn't happy with the way the items had been placed in the box. I tried my best to put forward my version of events and managed to squeeze $40, which for a fleeting moment felt like a huge win, but in reality, we'd been shafted.

Mum and Dad had no idea what I'd been through and I certainly wasn't going to tell them. They had utmost trust and faith in Miss Feneley and she had spun me the line for them, convincing me that the location of my first paid modelling gig would be acceptable to them. I swallowed Madame's assertion that all of these experiences would benefit me in the long run, and I didn't want my parents' strict and conservative values getting in the way.

I went back for more. Exposing me to more experiences became a mini-mission for Miss Feneley. Next stop: the military. Newcastle is a glorious harbour city in New South Wales and sighting the horizon usually involves counting ships awaiting their turn to dock. It's also been an important harbour for Australian naval ships and submarines.

Periodically there would be an occasion, usually on a Thursday or Friday evening, for Madame's selected few, the ones that had achieved a certain level of deportment and speech and stature – namely the ladies. There were a few gentlemen in our posse, ones who never spoke of their same-sex attractions, who occasionally accompanied us to an officer's cocktail party – a catered intimate party in the officer's mess on board the ship or submarine. We were there to provide some entertainment and light relief, presumably all while gaining valuable life experience. Hmmm...

I admit going on board the subs was pretty cool and I did get lots of practice in conversing with officers, who had minimal outside contact with non-commissioned people. I had entered the world of 'medium-height' society; acting, dressing and speaking like a lady. Descending stairs, sitting up straight, alighting vehicles, minding my manners, smiling and laughing on cue. But there was never was a conversation with my cohorts, or Madame herself, about what to do regarding consent or how far we should go in entertaining the officers, or how we would support each other if one of us felt awkward, uncomfortable, or unsafe.

One evening, while on a submarine, I began talking with an officer who was young enough to be interesting to me. Things were going well as we chatted in a small group, and later we talked some more on our own. Cocktail hour was generally from six to eight so, and as the hour of eight approached, he asked me if I'd like to join him and a few of the others for dinner onshore. He indicated that the 'others' included some of the posse I arrived with. I'd driven myself to the wharf, as had the other guests, so I agreed to the dinner invitation, and offered to drive the officer to the restaurant. He'd made a reservation at the Travelodge restaurant overlooking Newcastle Beach. All I expected was a lovely meal, views and conversation with adults – where I wouldn't be viewed as the child or the little sister, daughter, cousin or grandchild. I was seventeen – the confusing stage somewhere between a kid and a young woman. I parked in the basement car park and we caught the lift up to the restaurant. He gave his name and we were shown to our table. It was a table for two. I asked where the others were, and he told me they had a change of plans. Suddenly it felt like I'd taken a step in a new direction, or that I was led over a divide.

I didn't resist sitting down with him. I didn't make a stand and tell him I wanted to leave. I was okay about having dinner with him, although hesitant at the same time. I began to feel quite isolated and realised nobody knew where I was. He was very attentive, showering me with compliments on how I looked, my smile, and everything I said. A steady diet of soap operas throughout my life stood me in great stead for a moment such as this; the romantic ideal, dressing and behaving in a way that would attract 'the right man'. I figured this would add to my collection of great experiences that would in some way, someday, be a wonderful resource for my acting career. I wasn't quite prepared for what happened next. During our main meal he began to declare his love for me.

'I think I'm falling in love with you,' he said, to which I replied with a shocked exclamation, 'What? But you don't even know me. We've only just met!'

He kept going, carrying on with the compliments, and he went from 'thinking' to actually declaring his love for me. I tried to deflect the intensity of these declarations but the more I said, the more he seemed to love me! I told him I was happy to be friends with him, but I couldn't reciprocate his feelings.

As we were finishing dessert he told me he'd booked a room upstairs and insisted I come up and join him. I hesitated. It was getting late and the plan had been to have dinner with a group of people, drive my new friend back to the wharf and go home, not this. My parents understood I was out enjoying this social whirl, supposedly supported by a reputable 'agent', and others I knew. I had a midnight curfew. I was a virgin and had made my own decision to wait until I was eighteen before 'doing *it*.' I was also taught to be polite, not to disappoint, to do what was expected of me, and to be careful. I relied on humour and charm to get me out of harm's way, but I realise now that because of my humour and charm I've had a few close calls. This was one of them.

Reluctantly I agreed to go to his room, 'just to have a look', and made it very clear I was not staying over. He pleaded with me to stay longer, and to avoid saying 'no' and causing him to be disappointed, I agreed to stay for a cup of tea. Once in his room, things got pretty heavy and I felt really isolated now that I didn't have the perceived safety of the eyes of the waiting staff or restaurant diners. I was actually in this guy's hotel room within four hours of meeting him. We began kissing and he was holding me firmly. He kept going. I pulled back.

'No,' I said.

I wanted to get out of there. I wanted to run, but couldn't. I had to extract myself in my most friendly, charming and polite way, so as to minimise his disappointment and to maintain my pristine record of being a nice young lady. I did it. Closing the door to his room behind me, I walked as fast as I could to the lift, my heart racing. I was terrified going to my car in the basement, feeding the fears founded in my insatiable diet of American TV shows like *Starsky and Hutch* and *Charlie's Angels*. A woman alone in a car park at night never ends well. Looking all around me, I hastened my speed to the car. Even then I didn't feel safe. When I was finally at home in my own bed, I may have been safe at last, but I lay awake stressing over my close call.

The next morning the evidence, a long-lasting reminder of last night's experience, was obvious. A large bruise on my neck – my first 'love bite'. Mum was uncharacteristically ambivalent when she saw it and suggested I wear a scarf to try and hide it. That was about it. The end. I never discussed this character-building experience with Madame or any of the others who were with me at the cocktail party and interestingly not one of them enquired how my evening ended. One thing was certain: it was an experience I would not forget, I'd take it with me and it would be added to the collective library of experiences cross-referenced under 'close call,' 'near-miss,' 'creeps I've met' and 'fear of sexual assault'.

This library grew a lot in my time under Madame's 'guidance'. My classes with her continued, there were more social gatherings where her selected group were paraded before dignitaries and visiting officers. There were times we travelled to the RAAF base at Williamtown for similar functions and cocktail parties, but it was the Navy that put on the biggest show. One of my female friends pointed out the suntan mark on an officer's finger, his wedding ring removed in readiness for meeting women at the cocktail party. File under 'creeps I've met'.

I must have been meeting expectations, and Madame noticed. She arranged for my nomination as an entrant in the Miss Personality Quest 1983. This was a state-wide competition for young women not considered attractive enough for a beauty pageant, yet sufficiently attractive and articulate to put their personality on show before a range of local office bearers in a reputable international service organisation. Essentially, it was a fundraising initiative for a disability organisation which was supported by said service club. A meeting was arranged between two men from the the club and my parents. I was there too, a disempowered, silenced voice, while decisions were made as to what would be involved. I was assigned a caretaker and chaperone called Arthur, a married man and father of two who lived nearby. Arthur was an insurance salesman, his BMW reeked of green-apple deodoriser. It was Arthur's job to look after me and to drive me to meetings, functions and fundraisers. Occasionally, Arthur would pick me up at lunchtime, buy me a sandwich and drive me to a carpark overlooking Nobbys Beach or the harbour, and we'd talk about upcoming engagements. The pungent scent of green apple permeated my food, my clothing, my pores.

I helped organise a couple of fashion parades in restaurants as fundraisers and sourced prizes for a big raffle. Arthur stood at my side on the shopping strip of Main Road in Cardiff one Saturday morning, as I sold raffle tickets. Many of the locals were known to my family, from years of community and voluntary work Mum and Dad had done at church, school and sporting clubs. A short time later, Arthur hosted a barbecue for me at his place – an opportunity to demonstrate his contribution to the club's office bearers. He picked me up from my home and drove me to his place, arriving 45 minutes before the guests arrived. He invited me inside. His children were in the lounge room, his wife upstairs getting dressed. Arthur was physically attentive, touching my shoulder, guiding me by hand through different rooms to show me around. I had blind trust in this man who had been assigned to me. He had many qualities which I'd been led to admire in a husband. He was friendly, a self-starter, successful at his job, he had a good car, a family. I started to picture myself as the wife of someone like Arthur. This was the convention I'd been led to believe was my destiny.

The guests arrived and everyone was introduced before we made our way to the garden. Arthur made sure he and I were seated next to each other, on bench seats. I felt fabulous wearing my new red-and-purple floral halter-neck jumpsuit, teamed with a bright yellow, loose-fitting, unbuttoned short-sleeve blouse. The seating arrangement, combined with my outfit, meant that Arthur had unfettered access to my bare back, which he continued to caress throughout the entire meal. Nobody else knew what he was doing. We were sitting at the table with his wife and other older adults. Nobody flinched. Not even me. Not outwardly at least. My mind and heart were galloping in equal measure, yet my body was frozen. I couldn't believe he would do this to me, to his wife! As my thoughts raged I worked hard to remain physically calm. I didn't want to make a scene – I needed to be polite and charming. I was a nice young lady who was there to please and do a good job. I knew he was being sleazy and awful, but I didn't have the courage to stand up and say, 'Enough!' or, 'What the hell are you doing?' Or at the very least to excuse myself feigning illness. I sat through it fulfilling my role as dutiful entrant.

A short time later, Arthur was busted, but not for being an opportunistic sleazebag. Arthur had kept the butts from the raffle tickets which had the names, addresses and phone numbers of locals, and had contacted them to sell them insurance. Word got out and a meeting was held between two more senior representatives from the club and my parents. This time they were interested in what I had to say. They asked me direct questions. I knew nothing about the raffle ticket rort, but I did tell them some of what I knew about Arthur and his inappropriate and unwanted advances towards me.

Once again there had been no discussion by any responsible person about where I could go should things not be working out with my assigned caretaker and chaperone. The gentlemen, who were senior office bearers, were genuinely concerned and took my claims very seriously. Mum and Dad were concerned also, although a little quiet. We all agreed that Arthur would be removed from his role as my caretaker, and I never saw him again.

I did see out my journey of the Miss Personality Quest in the regional judging, which was held at a place known then as the Morriset Mental Hospital. My girlfriends came to watch me strut the catwalk in two lovely outfits and be interviewed by the smarmy MC, who announced the total amount of my fundraising efforts, and asked me some questions like, 'What do you hope for the future?' My response, along the lines of, 'A future of peace and happiness – where everyone gets along,' seemed to do the trick. The 'Miss Personality' gold sash I wore at all of the future fundraising events, as well as at the judgement, had a special place in my treasure archive, but has since been lost along the way. I was grateful I didn't win and didn't feel like I lost.

Thanks to Madame for another great life experience. I was on my way to becoming a great actress.

KEEPING UP APPEARANCES

It seemed my friends and acquaintances were content on the dole. Their long and frugal days were spent sleeping, creating, reading, fixing, researching about music, motorbikes, machines and artwork. I enjoyed their camaraderie and self-guided education of life, around and beyond the confines of tertiary education, provided an important and influential base for me to flit in and fly from. Underground music, fashion, and pop culture were a driving force to the everyday decision making. Op-shopping as a fashion and cultural choice was starting to take off, much to the chagrin of my mother. She was horrified at the thought of her daughter raking through second-hand clothes. She chastised me and my friends for wearing clothes reminiscent of her past, as the aspiration of keeping up with contemporary style was important to her. I'd spent four years at a private girls' school, years becoming a 'young lady' dressed in lovely fabrics and fashions from boutiques, and now here I was searching for second-hand threads, preferably black, which was near impossible in Newcastle. Buying anything black required a shopping adventure to Sydney. I tore ladders and holes in black ribbed tights and didn't hesitate to take scissors to my clothes, cutting out chunks or removing sleeves or collars, leaving frayed edges exposed. My behaviour caused so much alarm at home that Mum threatened to *burn* all of my clothes if I brought one more item home from an op-shop. We had huge shouting matches over it. I was all about freedom of expression and she was about suppression of expression.

'What will the neighbours think?' or, 'You weren't brought up to be like this!' was often said to stifle and smother me. I talked – and shouted – a lot about being accepting and tolerant of people different to us and not judging people by the way they looked or what they wore.

My friends wore heavily studded jackets, belts and wristbands and sported multiple ear-piercings. Their hair was dyed and gelled in gravity-defying styles, the girls wore lots of dark eye make-up and lipstick. We blended op-shop finds with boutique buys from a handful of edgy places that began to erupt on the conservative surface of the Newcastle fashion scene. Trips to Sydney would result in some fresh fashion loot; friends would venture to London, bringing back great stuff and a head full of ideas.

Finding out about the latest music releases took resourcefulness, and a keen eye and ear. There was a record store in Newcastle, Tyrells which later became Oscars, which sold our kind of music. They'd order imported records on request and the rest of the time the collective musical stock of friends was sourced from trips to Sydney, and mail order from the UK and US. We borrowed records from each other, under strict care instructions, to make tapes, and we had access to the alternative radio 2NURFM which was Newcastle Uni's station.

Double J was 'Sydney radio', which we couldn't receive in Newcastle, but we always tuned in on the car radio on the visits three hours south. I didn't have the 'luxury' of being on the dole, but from my standpoint, and in my experience, these were busy and exciting times. We were learning to navigate our way in a society that didn't offer us much and to some extent it didn't matter, because we wanted to be the instigators, we wanted to buck the system, we wanted the alternative. In many ways it built our resourcefulness. Following our passions took real dedication, time and research, and what money we had.

At home it was all about conforming and fitting in and doing what was expected. It was beige carpet and wallpaper, it was red-brick veneer and garden rockeries. It was still church on Sundays, visiting relatives and garden nurseries and never rocking the boat.

A good friend had recently lost his mum – his dad had died some years ago before I'd met him. He was nineteen and lived alone in the family home after his mum died. I think his brother lived there on and off, but largely he was on his own. It was Christmas and I asked Mum and Dad if it would be ok if I invited my friend to Christmas lunch, explaining his circumstance. They happily agreed and reminded me Mumma and the grandparents of my sister-in-law would also be with us. I picked up my friend from his place mid-morning and drove him back to mine. We had a curved driveway that led down to the front door – sheer aqua curtains allowed people inside to see out. I'm glad my family had those couple of minutes to prepare themselves for when we walked in.

My guest wore bleached patchy jeans and Doc Martens 12-hole boots. His jacket, wristbands and belt were all studded leather, and he wore multiple earrings and an eight-inch-high Mohawk tinted pink and green. He had beautiful twinkly blue eyes and a gorgeous grin. Mum and Dad welcomed him into our home, and to the table, and we all enjoyed a really wonderful meal. After lunch and chit-chat I drove him home. He'd had a really lovely time and thanked me. I was happy he was with us and didn't spend his first Christmas alone. When I arrived home, Mum, Dad and all the grandparents were singing the praises of my friend. They all thought he was a really lovely person – genuine and gentle; and there it was – proof to Mum that we have more to gain by giving people who are different to us a chance.

THE BEST YEAR OF MY LIFE

For decades I recalled the year I turned nineteen, 1984, as the best year of my life. A grand statement, especially since I've travelled the world and become a mother since then. Nonetheless, it's a statement that has stood the test of time. It was the year Mum and Dad left home. The awkward, emotional and confrontational decision for me to move out of home was taken away from me when Dad was transferred to Victoria for work. I'd been mothered to the point of being smothered, living under a strict regime that belied the times and my generation. I'd fallen in with the right crowd, for me, at the time. I seriously needed to bust loose. I cheerily waved Mum and Dad off; in fact, I can't even remember them leaving. My friend Donna moved into the family house with me until it was sold. We lived on Lambrusco wine, cheese, cabanossi and Jatz crackers. Up to this point I'd lived my life according to extremely high standards of cleanliness and tidiness, standards that fell to zilch within days. Oblivious to my responsibilities, I received my first bollocking from my brother. He popped in to check on the house during the week when we were at work, and was confronted by my pigsty. Apparently, the real estate agent was about to bring potential buyers through, and the state of the house was 'completely unacceptable'.

I got my shit together quickly, and Donna and I moved into town. We found a partly-furnished two-bedroom apartment on the ground floor of a Victorian-era building in King Street, on the border of Newcastle proper and Cooks Hill. It was grand, but also run down just enough to make it liveable and affordable. Without any fanfare, I bought a stack of kitchen supplies at the supermarket in my lunchbreak and set up house with Donna quick sticks. I could not wait to be free.

It was 1984 and Newcastle's independent and alternative music scene was thriving. We had a lot of choices between interstate, international and local bands, all of whom bucked the mainstream trends of the time. Nightclubs after midnight hosted drag shows and DJs, and we danced to New Order, The Cure, Culture Club, Madonna, Bronski Beat 'til the wee hours, several nights a week.

The venues didn't intimidate anyone and welcomed the misfits, outsiders and people experimenting with their identity, in search of their tribe or just a place to be that wasn't overrun by surfies, westies and yobbos. It was a really unique period of Newcastle's social history, largely unknown by the masses. We did buck the system from which we were alienated. It gave us cause to think and react independent of expectations, in a way where we followed our own lead. Of course, there were people pulling strings to bring us the venues and the bands and the exposure to this new way. There was a seedy underbelly, there was violence, hard drugs, sexism, racism, homophobia and a lot of risk-taking, prevalent throughout society in general, and at the same time, this subculture provoked our thinking towards some things and away from others. All of us who lived through this, not everyone made it, shared in something unique. There was an explosive creative scene that brought about a climate of acceptance and self-expression, mirroring the experiences in London and New York, in Sydney and in Melbourne, without orchestration. It was reactionary.

The fun and games continued. Two great girlfriends moved into the flat next door and we anticipated the arrival of our male mates at the sound of their Ducati, Moto Guzzi, Suzuki and Yamaha turning the corner. We could walk to wherever we needed to go – The Grand Hotel, the Blast Furnace, the Great Northern, Pipers, Night Moves, Jolly Roger, the Cambridge, the Palais, Newcastle Workers. We'd drive to the Doyalson RSL, Cardiff Workers, Norths and the Sixteen Footers to see our bands. Sometimes we'd go to Sydney, other times the hardcore fans from Sydney would come to Newcastle, for a laugh. The skinheads usually got into a fight, but largely we had the mods, rockers, punks, skins, and sixties-infused psych-pop-heads getting on. Hippies were given a bit of a hard time.

My hometown had its share of derision and self-loathing. There was a strong sense among my peers that Newcastle was a place we couldn't wait to get away from or we actually couldn't escape from. Unemployment was high in the early 80s – the steelworks was closing down and for the first time in generations, it was no longer a given that you'd get a job after leaving school. Uni was an option, and getting a trade at 'tech' was valued, especially if you could get an apprenticeship. Many chose the army, air force or navy as their ticket out. The gender divide in post-school options was significant with nursing, teaching or administration for females, and engineering or metallurgy being popular higher-Ed studies for males in Newcastle – among my peers at least. Academic pursuits were rarely mentioned out loud and therefore, I found them unimportant or at least unattainable.

My parents forged a clear plan for me, which went to (their) plan. I didn't finish my twelve-month secretarial course, instead they showed me an ad for an entry-level position as a typist/clerk at Civil & Civic, a construction subsidiary of Lend Lease. I'm still surprised that finishing my course wasn't considered important – there was a sense of urgency to attain employment. From this job I hopped and skipped to others, working continuously for five years, then I decided to study in Melbourne.

CHASING A DREAM

The start of 1984 was the time I've often claimed as my political awakening. I had a realisation I was a *white* Australian when walked through the door for an interview for the role of secretary to the state director of the National Aboriginal Conference, New South Wales. I got the job and was the only non-Aboriginal employee. During the following year, I was privy to many conversations about land rights, all of which had their roots in Terra Nullius – a misnomer based on the notion that the land which was to become Australia belonged to nobody. This period of my life, when my political views were shaped and informed by the world around me and not by my family and conservative education, has embedded within me a need to do more. My conviction has waxed and waned at times, but always returns. I call it my boomerang effect. My yearning to learn and understand my position, stepping forward and sideways isn't always comfortable yet I have struggled to let go. It won't let go of me.

It was late in the year when out of the blue I received a letter from Dad. It contained a newspaper clipping from Melbourne advertising the tertiary orientation program – the Year 12

Higher School Certificate equivalent – in *drama*! I couldn't quite believe that my dad had actually been listening to me all this time, I honestly thought he didn't hear me, didn't get me, didn't understand. For him to suggest this as an option – further education and drama studies – well, it was mind blowing. I sent off my application and started making plans to tidy up my life in Newcastle and head for Melbourne. It seemed like a perfect and natural fit. Mum and Dad had settled out of town, in Macedon, so the idea of living with them was not even possible. I made the most of my last months in Newcastle and when it came time to say goodbye the timing was brilliant. I had some of my best friends around me, some had already left and there were new faces emerging on the scene. Even though I didn't yet know if I'd been accepted into the course, I had blind confidence that something would work out. It was my logical next step. I'd packed up my life into boxes, the removalists arrived on a Friday and carted it to Melbourne. All I had left was the bed that came with the flat and my clothes and favourite things, which included my prize treasure, a life-size Elvis cardboard cut-out – all which would fit in the aqua Datsun 120Y Coupe my mum had loaned to me after she and Dad left Newcastle. What a little ripper of a car! That little sporty two-door had carried Mum and me to Townsville and back years before, and had made countless trips to Sydney, the Hunter Valley and then to Melbourne.

My last night in Newcastle, at my fabulous flat in King Street, was shared with Donna – my first ever flatmate, and a wonderful friend who taught me so much and who never cramped my style. Lots of friends came over, we went out dancing, came home late, then sat around talking for hours. I was jubilant with excitement and busting to take on the world. They were excited for me too, but even through my adrenaline rush I understood the feeling of saying goodbye to someone heading off on a new adventure, when ultimately things stayed the same for you, could be deflating. I know that things rarely stay the same, but for many of the people I left behind, things actually did stay the same. They went on with their jobs, or looking for jobs. Or maybe they moved house, changed housemates, found a job. Some big news would break for one of us – my friend scored a modelling gig and went to LA for six weeks, others went to London, some to Sydney, one spent a long time in Darwin, a couple went to Perth, some to the country, others just drifted off. Some got into heavy drugs, a few died. And so it went.

My friend Julie responded to the call I'd put out for someone to join me on the drive to Melbourne. She was the perfect companion. We hadn't known each other that long, but had crammed a lot of fun and parties and gigs into our short friendship. It was a new beginning and I didn't really need to explain much to her at all. It was a hot drive to Gundagai on 2 February 1985; we grabbed an onsite van at the caravan park, chosen purely because it had a pool. We spent hours floating about after a long day of driving.

In Melbourne, I stayed with friends of Michelle (who had helped me with the lingerie parade at the pub), P & K, a gay couple. Like me, they grew up in Newcastle and decided to bypass Sydney and head straight for Melbourne. We decided I'd be their welcome and appreciative housemate – I couldn't wait. I was about to turn 20, I'd uprooted my whole life, leaving everything I knew to embark on an unknown adventure. I still didn't know if I had been accepted for the course or not so, on a whim, I called the coordinator when I arrived in Melbourne and pleaded with her to let me in. It turned out that wasn't necessary. As a mature-aged student (at twenty years of age) I was in!

My new home was a two-bedroom apartment above a drycleaner in Carlisle Street, Balaclava. The place had a great layout and a fabulous rooftop garden, which I didn't appreciate at the time. P & K had injected character and beauty into that place. They were an intense couple who were passionate about opera and food and art and antiques and films and Esther Williams and chamber music and philosophy. We laughed enormously, they took great care of me and I'm sure I served as light relief. I relished our op-shopping trips together and was the recipient of many of their scores when they shopped without me. They could be as volatile as they were passionate, and as a couple they were complex. I witnessed too much violence between them, dealing with it by distracting myself, or them if I could, or offering comfort in the aftermath. The three of us were outsiders in a new city, muddling our way and following shimmery leads to find our tribe wherever we could.

The anonymity of arriving in a new city where nobody knew me was entirely liberating. I didn't have to explain anything I didn't want to, I could make my own decisions about everything, it was all up to me. I knew I wouldn't bump into anyone I knew, that I didn't have to behave in a certain way because someone might see me. I wasn't trying to impress a soul. I was finally free to be me. A favourite pastime was hopping on a tram and seeing where it would go, watching people and places from arm's length. I'd make up stories about people I saw, wonder where they bought their clothes, who they were going to see, where they worked, what they did. Could they want another friend? It sounds a bit stalker-ish by today's standards, but I was alone in a new and big city and if I saw someone I thought looked like they could be my friend, I'd get off at their stop, and watch, or maybe follow, just for a bit, to see what shop they went to. It was research.

The novelty of catching trains and trams for more than two hours a day, Balaclava to Preston and back, lasted quite a while, but in the end it was unsustainable. Plus I'd forged friendships with people who lived on the northside. I continued living with P & K while spending many nights on the couch of a friend in Thornbury, but the writing was on the wall and the time had come to move out of Balaclava.

Kim was my first friend in Melbourne. She had her shit together, was well connected and lived in a house she rented from her mum. She had her own dog and washing machine and car and she was a great cook! She studied drama with me five days a week and had a part-time job making cheesecakes and chocolate cakes in an industrial kitchen in a Fitzroy back street. Whereas I was effectively homeless, knew nobody, didn't have a car or a washing machine, let alone a job, and hardly knew my way around Melbourne. We instantly became great friends and laughed, cried, philosophised, wrote, argued and slept together. Until I met Andrew.

Sometime in the winter of 1985, Kim and I went to a party in Fitzroy. Turns out it was a big taco party, which meant a shared house packed with people in every room, loud music, beer, cider, pot and someone making tacos in the kitchen. It was a great night. I had the best time and spent it mostly in the kitchen. Oh, how I laughed and chatted and was typically charming to everyone in my path. What a hoot!

A couple of days later back at Kim's place her friend George wanted to bring his mate Andrew over. He was the guy from the party making the tacos and, apparently, I had charmed him and he wanted to see me again. Thing is, I didn't even remember meeting him at the party! I guess I was enamoured by the sound of my own voice as I sat perched on the kitchen bench, embracing the entire company of the kitchen.

Back in Kim's kitchen that Sunday afternoon, she and I sat drinking tea and chewing the fat; I'd been wondering if perhaps I should give guys a rest for a bit, and whether or not I should explore the girl-on-girl thing, when the doorbell rang. Completely unaware and unprepared for what was about to happen I just sat staring at the shadows on the floor. Hearing the crunch of the bamboo curtain beads I looked up and saw standing in the doorway, the most beautiful, tall man, wearing a black coat, big boots and a silver ring on his left hand. He smiled his captivating smile right at me. I don't remember ever seeing him before in my life but there he was, standing before me, just the two of us for a second that felt like it lasted a minute. Kim and George pushed their way into the kitchen and (re)introduced me to Andrew. We were both all smiles, laughing and talking and drinking tea and smoking pot. It was so easy! He was interested in everything I said, I asked him a thousand questions and we talked all afternoon, both of us oblivious to anyone else. Kim cooked dinner, we ate, we talked, we had another cuppa and it was getting late. He had to go.

Our courtship was slow and interrupted by a pre-arranged trip back to Newcastle, my first homecoming since I'd left for Melbourne at the beginning of the year. Our first serious action session of lips and tongues and absolute passion took place in the bus terminal in Franklin Street at my departure. I promised to write to him, which I did. Those two weeks away were really what I needed to affirm my choices and contentment with the new life I was carving in Melbourne. Even though I was still relatively homeless, still crashing on Kim's couch, my belongings in her shed, without a job, I was living my dream, studying drama. It was wonderful to see my friends again. I stayed for a week in my old flat in King Street with Donna and the following week in Sydney with a much-loved friend Tracy – she'd made the break from Newcastle a couple of years before. She was living my Sydney dream for me. For a range of reasons, I never sent that letter I'd written to Andrew. I also couldn't ring him – no phone at King Street and a shared house phone in Sydney made it more complicated than it should've been. The day before I was due to return to Melbourne, I called Kim to let her know the time my bus was arriving. All she could talk about was what a great guy Andrew was, how much she liked him, how much time they'd spent together. I felt sick with jealousy. It was a long trip back with the sound of her voice reeling inside my head. I felt so nervous as I got off the bus in Flinders Street. Grabbing my bag from cargo I looked up and saw Kim and Andrew walking together, laughing, their shoulders and arms touching. I was furious, but I knew I had no right. I played it cool and just said 'hi', then he kissed me and he held my hand, and I knew for sure. Once we eventually got it on, it was on.

After months of couch-surfing at Kim's I plucked up the guts to move out and found a shared townhouse with three male strangers in North Melbourne. I can't even remember their names. Basically, it was a place I could have my stuff after taking it out of storage, a place I could enjoy the privacy and luxury of housemates who did not know everything about me.

One morning after a wonderful night together, Andrew and I lay dozing in a still and empty house. Whoever they were, my housemates had all gone off to work or uni or whatever it was they did. It was about 10am and I'd made the decision a few hours earlier to give school a miss for the day. I felt a bit bad because we had a dress rehearsal for our community theatre piece, and it's extremely poor form to miss a rehearsal, let alone the dress rehearsal. I just couldn't get out of bed. I'd found paradise, and he was lying with me in my bed and the gravitational pull was greater than any sense of responsibility I had to my fellow actors. This was serious. Suddenly the phone rang and as I clomped down the stairs to answer it I realised it could be my director wanting to know where I was. Within those last few steps I decided it would be best if I pretended to be a cleaner who would not really be able to understand what was going on, because she would be… Spanish! At this point in my life, my only exposure to a Spaniard had been Manuel from *Fawlty Towers*, or Charo, a regular B-grade celebrity who appeared on *The Love Boat* – in fact I think she's actually Mexican. Doesn't matter, cos in my best Charo accent, I answered the phone, 'Hello!'

'Hello, can I speak to Karen please.' It was my director.

'No, no, no – Karen is not here! I don't know where she is, I am the cleaner. Sorry!'

With that bold-faced lie, I hung up and ran upstairs, dying with shame and embarrassment as I told Andrew what I'd done. The look of shock and astonishment on his face made me realise what a stupid fucking thing I'd just done.

The next day Kim recalled what happened in the theatre after my director had spoken to me on the phone.

'You are in big trouble Karen – what were you thinking?'

'Really? What did she say?'

'She told us, "Well everyone, Karen won't be in. I've just spoken to her and she pretended to be the cleaner!"'

Needless to say, I failed that particular subject. However, I came through with flying colours on everything else. And that is the best and only story to come from my time in that North Melbourne house.

My acting dream didn't pan out the way I'd envisaged – so say 90 per cent of trained actors, and it was true for me. After a year of being an impoverished and hungry student in a new city, with insecure housing, coming within a hair's breadth of begging for a meal on Brunswick Street, I realised if I was to get any acting work it would have to be in addition to working 'a real job'. I had to prioritise regular paid work. I had a few bar jobs, worked as a sandwich hand, but I resisted the skills in which I was really trained and where I had experience: administrative/secretarial work. It seemed like a step backwards and a distraction from realising my artistic dream. To satiate my unmet desire to perform, create and act, for the next twelve years or so I managed to engage with at least one major production a year through youth arts festivals and theatre companies.

GETTING READY

I'd spent the best part of three years off work due to a repetitive strain injury and my days were filled with appointments with physiotherapists, masseurs, doctors, psychologists and occupational rehab. Considering the uncertainty and the chronic pain, I coped reasonably well. Because of the lack of physical appearance of injury, I needed to justify each time I was referred to a new clinician. Repetitive Strain Injury (RSI) was a fairly new phenomenon in 1987 and, like many invisible chronic pain conditions, it's often met with suspicion, if not overlooked completely.

I didn't want to be overlooked, I wanted to be seen and heard in a conservative and increasingly hostile environment. My hair was long with a massive undercut and a peace sign cut into it, I pulled and sometimes pushed a red vinyl trolley about the city as carrying bags of shopping was really difficult due to my injury. I was politically awakened and took absolute exception to the violation of Indigenous rights to land and culture in this country. I was rightly suspicious of law and order, and particularly that which stemmed from US occupation of sovereign lands, and the covert operation in Pine Gap. I marched against Jeff Kennett's contempt for public health and education and closures of schools and hospitals, and I marched and shouted against the invasion of Iraq by allied forces. It could be said I was pissed off, and the stickers on my red vinyl shopping jeep shouted as much.

In my downtime I offered to help Andrew's band get a lot more organised and entered the rock 'n' roll arena as a proactive band manager/publicist. I taught myself and found myself along the way, cold-calling and bar-tapping at venues, calling bookers and bands trying to get better gigs, better deals and create a vibe. It was the late 80s in Melbourne and the free street press was just taking off. The obsession with cover bands was loosening its hold on inner-city venues and there was a lot of burgeoning action to be found at The Tiger Lounge, the Creole Club, The Central Club, The Club, the Richmond Club, The Corner Hotel, The Punters Club and The Evelyn. Public radio (at least Kennett hadn't attacked that!) was the best in the world, arguably with 3RRR FM the leading light. It saved my sanity and pushed my brain into unchartered terrain, for which I'll be forever grateful, at a time when the outside world appeared hostile.

I started to make a difference to the numbers at gigs and the number of gigs around town, and people started to notice. This was my own form of rehabilitation, and the gratis work I did for the band gave me a reason to get out and talk to people. That time and effort paid off in spades when I scored a job away from the shackles of WorkCover and within a new scene, a place I didn't realise existed, where you could work and be paid to follow a passion. The music industry had become a passion of mine, not just as a spectator, supporter and consumer, but as a participant, a contributor. My new gig with The Push was working on a program called the Rock Music Support Service – we provided resources and advice to young bands trying to get their music out to the world. I made some lifelong friends during this time, and others who would fade in and out and back in again. But no matter what I did or wherever I went, a shapeless cloud followed me, the one containing my unknown truth.

∞

IT WAS THE DAWNING of a new decade. The 90s. Mum and I spent the day together in Melbourne. We stood on the corner of Swanston and Little Collins waiting for the lights to change. She asked me if Andrew and I had talked about having children.

'Of course not, because I have no plans to have children,' I was quick to respond.

She asked if we were happy together.

'Yes,' I replied definitely and definitively. The last five years together had been amazing and although nothing was written in stone, I couldn't imagine my life without him. Actually, sometimes I did imagine my life without him; a kind of mental/emotional insurance policy, imagining that I could cope quite well without the love of my life. I know there are no guarantees with life and one day maybe I would find myself alone.

Absolutely, positively, I knew that Andrew and I were meant to be together. Yes, we were happy. Then out of the blue, on one of the busiest street corners in Melbourne, Mum asked, 'Would you like to look for Ann?'

A resounding thump resonated between my heart and my head. This was what I'd waited to hear, knowing full well I'd struggle to bring this up myself. Mum was always the one who I thought needed protection – she was vulnerable, sensitive and used her emotional pull to sway my behaviour and thinking. She had a hold over me. I'd always explained it away as the desperate love she had for a daughter for whom she longed, for so long. Whose arrival was met with much expectation, that her imaginings of a life with a daughter were laden with her own visions of what a perfect mother-daughter relationship would be; the perfect relationship she wasn't able to have with her own mother.

Now that she'd asked me the question, I had permission to unlock a part of my heart which had only dared to dream of the possibilities. I'd been forever captured within my own mind, fantasising about the possibilities; the practicality of making it happen hadn't fully occurred to me.

'Yes,' I said. 'I am ready.'

The lights turned green and together we crossed the road.

∞

IN 1992, MUM AND I started putting feelers out on how, what and where we needed to go to find Ann. It was a long process that started with a phone call, then paperwork, phone calls, a few more forms, bit payments here and there. The process was complicated by the fact that Andrew and I were heading off on a big trip. We weren't sure how long we'd be gone, but we had twelve months until our around-the-world tickets expired. Before we left I completed a host of other forms and advised the authorities I'd registered with of the changes to my contact details while travelling. There were a few little nibbles of information before we left, although nothing substantial. At the same time, I was encouraged and felt like I was getting closer to some greater discovery – as well as the big trip.

Andrew and I kicked off our world tour in Bali then headed for the United Kingdom, Europe and the US. England was so much like home, simultaneously comforting and exciting. Mum and Dad have always been staunch royalists and it was hard to get beyond the fact we were in the Queen's own country. I'd always been enthralled by royalty and the lineage of family that was so easily traceable. The museums, castles, towers, bridges and cathedrals were an endless source of fascination as I absorbed the history of this crazy and affluent family, with its origins, branches and evolution. It fed my fantasies of finding my own family tree.

Nothing quite prepared me for what I experienced in Europe.

Travelling on the long train journey from Paris to Rome, I found myself stretching and wandering up the corridor as we snaked and curled around the foot of the Alps towards the border. Around the point where the guards changed from French to Italian I was suddenly confronted by several people who spoke to me in Italian. Dissatisfied with my explanation that I was not actually Italian, they gesticulated even more, questioning me. I did my best to assure them I was Australian and couldn't understand what was going on. Arriving back in my seat I tried to make sense of it with Andrew. It dawned on me that I actually looked Italian. Even the Italians thought so! I was shocked, yes, but mostly I felt reassured and a sense that I was welcomed and could see myself belonging somewhere other than an Anglo-centric society.

These feelings were amplified wherever we went in Italy – I didn't force it or question it, instead I allowed it to wash over me and made a vow that one day I would return when I knew more. As a visitor to many places the experiences speak out in different ways. We travelled to Scotland by road, joined by Andrew's brother, his partner and their adorable two-year-old daughter, traveling down narrow roads, motorways, along fjords and hills in a Fiat van towing a trailer tent. There were some hairy moments when that load wasn't going to make it up a hill without us disembarking, running, pushing, then jumping back in. I was really looking forward to Scotland – it was the place of my family's folklore, I was a Forbes, I grew up knowing the family tartan. Our motto 'Grace Me Guide' was displayed on brooches, placemats, spoons and even our door knocker. Andrew's dad was born in Aberdeen, the region of the Forbes clan. There was always a plan to visit the house where he grew up before he'd left his country and kin at the age of sixteen to set sail for the world and a lifetime at sea in the merchant navy. I understand the imposing harbour and ships from around the world on the city's doorstep would have held an irresistible lure to an adventure-seeking young man in wartime Scotland, an escape to the wild, blue yonder. From my family's standpoint, Scotland remained largely an unattainable place belonging in yesteryear, the place from which great-grandfather Forbes left to find a better life, unaware of the yearning his descendants would have for his land or origin. Scotland has always been built up in my mind to hold the stories and the keys to a greater familial belonging that could never be matched in Australia. I was ready.

Andrew had been given the address of the house of his father before we left, but I hadn't given it much thought until the day came when we went to find the house. Unfolding the piece of paper, we saw the name of the street we were looking for was Forbes Street, Aberdeen. I couldn't believe this connection between our two families had never been made before and I took it as a wonderful omen – so it would be our families were linked, were tied.

THE FILE

When I was in my twenties, Mum handed me an old, worn envelope marked 'Confidential Papers'. I recognised it from when I was young, around the time she told me Ann's name and that my biological father was Italian. She'd had it ever since I arrived in her arms at one month of age, with the expectation the day would come when she would hand it to me. For all those years she was quietly preparing herself for the right time. These papers held something more than stories. They provided tangible evidence, records of what I'd been told was true.

It included the cardboard nametag that had been tied to my infant wrist by the nurse who delivered me to Broadmeadow station on 8 of March 1965, and some maternal health records with my mum's handwriting declaring that 'Karen would be attending our family doctor' and not the one assigned by the government. Due to my 'ill health' as a baby (the mild talipes which resulted in my legs being plastered from the knees down), my formal adoption was deferred and I was officially a Ward of the State – in the care of my new family. This carried an added element of concern for my parents, Mum in particular.

Worn and aged papers and cards had been thoughtfully kept – the first pieces of the puzzle that was my heritage.

Two separate social workers' records were in the envelope, notated at different times, based upon information provided by my birth mother. It's impossible to tell what state Ann was in when she gave this information. She was an unmarried pregnant woman in 1964/65 living in relative isolation in a boarding house in Sydney. Her father was the only person who knew of her pregnancy, and made all the arrangements for his daughter to relinquish her baby. It's possible he may have provided some of the information to the social workers. I'll never know.

---

31 March 1965

Dear Mrs Forbes, I have pleasure in confirming the placement of Baby McGarry in your care as a ward of this Department (Child Welfare Department). The following details concerning this child may be of assistance to you.

Full Name of Ward: McGarry (female)

Date of birth: 8.2.65

Religion: Approval has been given to baptise the baby in the Church of England faith. It would be appreciated if you would arrange to have this carried out at your earliest convenience and forward a copy of the Baptismal Certificate to this office when completed.

Also included were further details of immunisation requirements. Mum's writing at the bottom of this letter reads,

'Karen was always taken to Dr Muller, never to the "Local Council Scheme".'

---

17 February 1966

I have pleasure in informing you that an Order of Adoption in relation to BABY McGARRY (Female) was made in your favour by the Supreme Court in its Equitable jurisdiction on the 10th February 1966 and that all legal formalities are now complete...

...This occasion cannot be allowed to pass without expressing thanks for the care and attention given to Karen during the time she has been with you. The Department does much for its wards, but it is the foster parents who provide them with the care and sense of security which means so much to children. It is hoped that the future will reward you both when you see Karen continuing to develop into the daughter of whom you will be proud.

Mum and Dad had attended a seminar for adoptive parents in Newcastle in 1976 and made some enquiries about my parentage. A reply arrived from the Department of Social Work, The Women's Hospital (Crown Street). It read as follows:

---

20 April 1976

... I have looked up the records and as you know I am unable to give you any

> identifying information however, the
> baby's mother was a 21 year-old lass,
> who had just completed first year at
> university. She was 5'4 1/2' in height,
> black hair, grey-green eyes, and fair
> complexion. She was of British ancestry,
> her health was good and so was that of
> her family generally. The baby's father
> was in his middle twenties, about 5'7' in
> height, dark brown hair, brown eyes and
> light olive complexion. He had reached
> Intermediate certificate standard and was
> working in the tailoring trade, and again
> his health was good, and that of his
> family.

The file grew and grew over the years. Its first big addition was my own doing in 1992, following my initial enquiries to find Ann. I received a letter from the Department of Family and Community Services (NSW), providing me this version of my heritage:

> Your mother Anne (misspelled) was 21 years
> old, had studied pharmacy at university
> for two years and then worked as a
> pharmacy assistant. She needed to support
> herself financially. She said your father
> was 26, an Italian whom she did not tell
> of her pregnancy. He was 5'7' tall, had
> brown hair, brown eyes and a light olive
> complexion. He had been in Australia for
> four years, was a tailor by trade but
> worked as a tracer/designer for a marble

company. He played the guitar. He had four brothers and three sisters. His father was a wholesale merchant.

Anne's father was a pharmacist, her mother worked in the shop. She had one brother, still at school, two sisters at school and one sister who worked as a receptionist. Anne was 5'41/2' tall, of slim build, with dark brown hair, blue-grey eyes and a fair complexion. She was described as very attractive and 'a fine type of girl.' She was interested in music and played the piano.

Both Anne and your natural father whom she did not name, were healthy…

TWO HUNDRED YEARS AGO... WHO WAS I?

I was taken away from my mother immediately after I was born. Government and social policy of the time meant it was near impossible for an unmarried mother to care for her own child. Without opportunity for employment, education and housing, my mother, like many women, had only one option that was pitched as being in the 'best interest of the child' at the time. That is, to give away her baby to a stable Christian couple who would offer more than she ever could. This option was the reality. Stigma for unmarried mothers in the mid-twentieth century was rife and so difficult to overcome, that very few did.

I was brought up in a home full of love, always knowing that I was dearly wanted and longed for by my adoptive parents. Knowing I was adopted, I had a happy childhood and grew up in a loving family, learning about family history, and taking it upon me as if it was truly my own. Always curious about my ancestors, I questioned my mother, my grandmothers and aunties endlessly about life in the olden days, enquiring about the names of everyone in the family as far back as they could remember. I embodied this Scottish and third-generation Australian ancestry and if I am to tell you who I was 200 years ago, it would probably have something to do with being a young girl running through fields of heather in the Scottish Highlands dreaming of an escape to a more sophisticated city full of churches and schools and structure. Or maybe the story would be about an uneducated young girl growing up the youngest in a large family on a farm in the Hunter Valley, New South Wales whose closest allies were the horses, cows and chickens. Or possibly my story would have been about a daydreaming farm girl who snuck away from her ever-present, over-bearing family whenever she could, to play and laugh with the Aboriginal children who lived on the banks of the river.

The devastation of learning of my Italian ancestry as a naïve, sheltered and coddled eight-year-old Anglo-Australian sent my head and heart spinning like tops in opposite directions. My reference points to Italian culture had been limited to the overworked owners of the local takeaway. I was not having any of it.

All of my life I have lived and learned the ancestry of a family in which I actually don't belong. This ancestry is not true. It is not mine. These feelings continue to challenge me and it's where I draw my inspiration. I re-imagine myself two hundred years ago as a woman surrounded by art, music and beauty in the stony surrounds of an Italian hillside village, overlooking the bluest sea, the air around me filled with sounds of laughter and the smell of food at a vibrant celebration.

The reasons for me being drawn towards the lived experiences of Aboriginal Australians are complex. My interest intensifies periodically, like a surge of energy from an unknown source. I've only recently begun to question this. At no time would I compare my experience with the impacts of colonisation and I acknowledge my inherent (inherited) privilege of being a white woman from a middle-class background. As I explore my own issues of identity and belonging, I understand some soft parallels exist between my experience and that of Aboriginal Australians whose family disconnections have been a result of enforced public policy. Still, I'm compelled to address injustice and feel duty bound to learn, understand and contribute towards a greater understanding of colonialism's impact on our nation's First Peoples.

I've attended many Welcome to Country ceremonies, conducted by respected Elders, and listened to stories by Aunties and Uncles who have been so generous with their time, knowledge and spirit. I'm deeply interested in ritual, which is why I became a practicing civil celebrant, authorised by law to marry two people, and I'm proud of the rituals I create with others to mark life's milestones – from birth to death. I've learned about the richness of culture, tradition, ceremony and ritual that underpin not only the day to day lives of traditional owners but their connection to past, present and future. I'm learning the ways in which culture, traditions and ceremony are crucial to the wellbeing of peoples who have been disconnected from their lands, waterways, animals, plants, culture, and language, and especially for all who live with the trauma of their experiences. Looking on with respect and fascination, I'm in awe of what I understand so far about the ritual and ceremony associated with possum skin cloaks. The process of women making a cloak for a pregnant woman's unborn child – a cloak that is allowed to grow with the child into adulthood, all the while mapping the life's journey within – is one of the most impressive rituals I know.

Journeying around Ireland many years ago, before I knew anything of my Irish ancestry, brought about a familiar sense of being and as I was cradled in the soft rain, the moors and the peat, the impact of the stories, song and history of this place took me by surprise. We ventured into cities, towns and villages, in stone circles and up cobblestone paths, and every step, every breath was like I'd experienced nowhere else. Such sadness and such joy, such despair and yet, hope. Acceptance and belonging. I felt at home.

A short time afterwards, travelling by train from France to Italy, I was mistaken as Italian once we'd crossed the border. The foreign language, sights, smells and tastes – the dry heat, the cobblestones imprinted with centuries old footsteps soaked into my blood stream. Could this place, two hundred years ago, have been my home? Could the ancestors of these people, two hundred years ago, have been my family?

How can it be possible to feel such a connection to so many places? At home I feel at home. Newcastle is my home, Sydney is my city, I choose Melbourne out of everywhere in the world. I'm connected to the land, trees, seas and roots of Australia. How can I be all of this?

COMING HOME

After six months of travelling we were ready to come home, I was ready to get on with the next chapter and felt a sense of urgency about what was waiting for me. After eight years of living in Richmond we moved further south to Windsor. A place where I felt sure new memories would be made that would be different from the past. We set up house and for a few months I was able to get some work back at The Push while a good friend was setting up his own artist management business.

At home we played hard – parties, gigs, dinners out and big sleep-ins. Weekend days were for sleeping and nights for living large. Windsor was thriving with twenty-four-hour pizza, video stores, bottle shops and quality restaurants and venues within an easy stagger. The Continental was our favourite and before too long I had a permanent gig at Smartartists and was working my passion – promoting music and attending gigs.

It was 1994 and I'd not lost sight of my acting dream; I was racking up many 'experiences to become a great actress'. The words of Miss Feneley still rang in my head, all these years later. I signed up for a year of study at the National Theatre Drama School (NTDS) in St Kilda. Two nights a week at drama school, five days a week at Smartartists office, weekly yoga class and several dinner dates and gigs; life was full to the brim. I had committed to a major production, several showcases for the year with an option to continue into year two and three. Studying kept my skills honed, my mind and body in tune and ready for characterisation for storytelling. I loved every minute – it kept my creative urges satiated.

This was the same year as my work exposed me to the world, words and minds of American spoken-word performers Karen Finley and Jon Giorno. I was inspired to push the envelope in my theatre studies, which was possibly my downfall in what at the end of the day was a conservative environment. Or maybe I could consider my final assessment – where I was encouraged to leave the school and 'just go out there and do it' – as permission to follow my heart's desire. There was nothing more NTDS could offer me, I just needed to go out there and do it. A frightening concept.

One night, Kim came over for a big night and sleepover catching up on what we'd missed over the past year. While there were overseas tales to recount, she really wanted to know if I'd had any news about finding my birth mother. As the night wore on, we ate, we drank, we smoked, and I showed her the copy of Ann's original birth certificate, which had recently arrived. The day I opened that envelope was the day a weighty coin dropped into the pit of my stomach. I got to read her name for the first time. I could see the names of her mother and her father, my grandparents. I could work out their ages and, in my mind, map the places they'd lived at the times of their marriage and Ann's birth. They were from Newcastle. Not Sydney. I had a long-held assumption that because I was born in Sydney that her family would be from Sydney. It never occurred to me that they would be from anywhere else. The most remarkable thing was that her place of residence had been in Wrightson Avenue, Bar Beach. The same street as my boyfriend Tim, with the driveway where I spent most weekends throughout my seventeenth year. I really was from Newcastle! This was monumental.

Kim suggested we call Directory Assistance on 013 – where a real life, locally based person could match a phone number to a last name, initials and suburb or town. They were not permitted to provide addresses or privately listed numbers. According to the dates on Ann's birth certificate, there was a twenty-year age difference between her father and her mother, and I presumed the father would be long gone by now. But I thought it may be possible to locate the number of Ann's mother, my grandmother. So I did. It was after midnight when I dialled 013. I gave the operator the name of my maternal grandmother and location as Bar Beach in Newcastle. Her search came up with nothing. When I explained what I was doing she offered to look further, across Newcastle and the Hunter Valley. She spent a few moments, holding me on the line as she searched. And then… a match! I now had my grandmother's name and a phone number. Thanking the operator, I hung up and stared into space, shocked. I had no intention of doing anything with this information immediately. Carefully, I put the number aside for safe keeping, for another day.

FINDING ANN

Not long after I stood at my phone table in my hallway, barely breathing as I first heard the words of my mother read by the lovely woman at the Post Adoption Resource Centre, I was holding a copy of Ann's letter. I would return often to these four handwritten pages by my birth mother. No matter how many times I read them, nothing quite compared with hearing her words for the first time. So many questions ran through my head when I heard and later read Ann's words as she asked: 'Did she die? Was she institutionalised? Why wouldn't anyone tell me what had happened to her?'

It appears it took twenty-one years after my birth for Ann to be informed what had happened to me. All she knew about me after my birth was the adoption was deferred until I was medically fit. She knew nothing else. She didn't even know if I had been adopted at all. She wanted to know if my condition, whatever it was, had been successfully treated. Ann wrote in her letter of her hopes that the relinquishing mothers of today would not be 'subjected to the same anguish (unnecessary and inhumane as I have been).'

She went on to write that after my birth she was transferred to the aftercare annexe for relinquishing mothers and had been administered drugs to suppress lactation.

With gratitude she anticipated a full and frank reply from the Department in what she called 'the enlightened eighties' and closed with:

```
I've often wondered what difference the
availability of supportive parents benefit
in 1965 would have made to my life —
and hers, but I'm sure I made the right
decision — in theory anyway — at the time
and in the circumstances.

Yours sincerely, Ann
```

After hearing the words of my birth mother read aloud by a stranger, I hung up the phone and sobbed. My head was spinning, my heart palpitating. My first response was to call Mum and tell her what had happened.

'Oh darling, what can I do?' she responded after I told her in a completely muddled way what had just happened. I had no idea what I wanted her to do, I'd only thought as far as telling her what had happened. There was no plan. She could hear the pain in my cries and even though she was just at the end of the line, her arms were an eternity away. I wanted her to help me.

'Mum I have this number, it might be Ann's mother.' I hesitated.

Without missing a heartbeat, she said, 'Give it to me and I'll ring it.'

I wasn't ready for this. But I was so ready for this. I gave her the number. She said she'd call me straight back. Her voice sounded uncharacteristically solid, propelled by a strength which was what I needed to support my quivering core. Now what? I had to wait for her to call me back. What was going on? Would she find out anything? How long would it take? I stared at the phone. I needed something. I put the kettle on. I went to the toilet. I came back and stared at the phone. The whistle blew, the phone rang.

'Mum!'

'Are you ready for this?'

'What? What?'

'Yes it was her and I have Ann's number.'

'What? How did you do that? What did you say? What happened?'

Mum asked the woman she spoke to if she was Ann McGarry's mother, to which she replied she was. Then Mum, my mum, came out with… 'My name is Barbara McDonald and I went to school with Ann.'

'Barbara McDonald? Mum, where did that come from?'

'Wait… guess what she said?'

'I have no idea!'

'She said, "Oh you were at Newcastle Grammar with Ann?" Karen, I nearly fell over!'

So did I! Another bombshell to follow the ones from the birth certificate. And so it was that I went to the same school as my birth mother. I had unknowingly traced her steps, touched the same walls, doorways and desks in some cases. My fantasies were closing in. But the fantasies I'd written for myself never involved a woman with whom I would have shared physical spaces.

'Karen, I have Ann's number. She lives in Tasmania. I'm going to call her now.'

Again with this confident, assured and caring voice. She was looking after me.

'Ok, if you're sure.' I quivered.

'I'll call you back.'

In a winding series of soap-operatic moments to rival the best of *The Young and the Restless*, an intense wait was ahead. I stared long and deep at the telephone and then out my lounge room window until my eyes welled. I walked to the stove, relit the kettle, staring until the whistle screamed. The water bubbled and waves of steam flooded my face while I poured over a teabag into my comforting pottery mug I had used since the seventies. I turned to look at the cigarette packet, rarely touched in daylight hours, slid one from the packet into my mouth and lit it up. I drew back, held and exhaled, took a sip of tea. Turning, I stared at the phone and back through the window. Still in my dressing gown, the waft of tea steam and cigarette smoke gave rise to the headiness of the occasion. I searched for tissues. The tightness in my throat gave me an earache. I had a headache, my heart ached. How long has it been? I looked at the clock, the phone, the window, took a drag, a sip and I sat. I stood up and paced, stared out the window, back at the phone, took a drag. The clock, window, phone, ciggy, tea. Phone, window, clock. Phone. Window. Window. Window.

An hour passed.

Are they ok? Are they crying? What if they're shouting? What if there's bad news? What if they hate each other? I hope they're ok? I really wanted them to be ok. I was so grateful they could have this moment together. Hopefully they could say what they needed to say. I don't need to be there. From one mother to another. To say what they needed to say. To get a sense that the other is alright. That their daughter is ok. Their daughter. They share a daughter. Me.

Forty-five more minutes passed.

The phone rang.

'Mum are you ok?'

'Well... I spoke with Ann.'

I wanted to know everything I could, I wish I could've listened in.

'Yes. What did you say? Was she ok? Was she shocked?'

'She answered the phone and I asked her if that's Ann and did she have a baby girl on the 8th of February 1965. She replied really quickly and said yes and then asked, "What did you call her?"

"Karen Ann," I said.

"Ann with an 'e' or without?"

"Without."

"Oh, thank you so much," she said, and it went from there.'

Mum couldn't tell me much more about what they spent an

hour and forty-five minutes talking about. Apparently it was a bit of who's who and when and where have you lived, that kind of thing.

'Does she have any other children?' I was desperate to know.

'Yes, she has two daughters and a son.'

Beaming, I said, 'I have sisters!'

'Yes.'

Mum gave their names and ages, and this information alone sets off my dreaming, imagining my parallel life growing up the oldest of four, in a family of three girls and a boy. The girls went to university. I didn't. They must be really bright. Ann told Mum about her own siblings and also that apart from her partner David, nobody knew about me. She'd never told her sisters, her brother or even her mother. It was her father who made all the arrangements for the adoption. I can't believe that her father wouldn't have told his wife that their daughter gave up her baby. Ann would need some time to process this and thanked Mum for her discretion when speaking with her mother. She definitely wanted to be in contact with me and would work out a way in which we could speak over the phone. In the meantime, she was happy to receive a letter and photos from me and would also send me some photos.

What a relief. My thoughts and feelings were entwined into an enormous ball of brain, heart and stomach hyperactivity. I was finally hungry, but couldn't think of eating. I needed a shower, but could barely move. So I wrote.

For you, For Me

Today I have found you
The mother in my dreams
I love you so much
My search is over yet another begins.
I know where you are
And that you are of this world
My world.

To hear your own words today
Was the most overcoming of all
For the first time I could imagine your voice, your thoughts
You didn't forget me.

I feel angry at the pain you have suffered
The unknown you have experienced
I had my own pain too
And it was also unknowing.

I am sad to think of the special moments we missed together
Yet overjoyed at the shiny, hopeful prospect for the future
I was terrified that I'd be too late to know you
I cried and cried – 'Please don't be dead.'

Thanks to my mum for using her imagination and determination
Out of her love for me
To take the risks and handle the consequences
I love you.

I felt a strong bond between four women
Ann, Doris (Enid), Barbara and Karen
Four strangers, bound by a secret love
And connected by telecommunications
A secret no more
I want the WORLD to know

I have to know you first
The world can wait
But I can wait no longer for you

Tuesday, 8th March 1994
29 years since I was delivered to Barbara and Ian
28 years since I was adopted by them
Today Mum and I found Ann
International Women's Day 1994

CONNECTING

Mother's Day came around and Andrew and I had planned to visit Mum and Dad in Macedon for lunch. I woke up early that morning with the worst gastro I'd had since Bali. Every time I moved I needed to poo and the pain was excruciating. There was no way I could manage the drive to Macedon. I rang Mum and told her we couldn't make it, which I knew would really disappoint her – part of the responsibility of being the child living in closest proximity. But she sounded more than disappointed. It wasn't so much sad, defeated or neglected as an enthusiastic disappointment. It turned out Mum and Ann had arranged for Ann to call me at Mum's place after lunch, for our first phone call. Oh no! Mum asked me if I wanted Ann to call me at home. I honestly didn't know if I could be compos mentis enough to have my first ever conversation with my birth mother while in agony with gastro. I really thought it was a bad idea, but Mum persisted, saying it would be really special being Mother's Day.

Ann called. I was writhing around on the futon lounge we'd extended in the lounge room. Desperately wanting to create a fabulous impression, I used every ounce of energy and courage to pull myself together. I could barely sit up and struggled to comprehend, be present, take notes and absorb the enormity of the moment. Hearing Ann's voice for the first time wasn't surprising. It was a voice I'd never heard before, but it was familiar. I was full of acceptance. Of her voice, her words, her story, her situation. My arms and heart were open within seconds. I completely surrendered to her, and then, I pulled back. I didn't want to be hurt, I didn't want her to not like me, to reject me, but ultimately, I didn't want to upset her. I have no idea what I would do that would ever upset her – I was, along with Mum, very careful not to impose upon her life, not to expect anything from her apart from a chance to know each other. I wasn't about to move into the family or blurt out her secret to the world.

Her first words to me were, 'What took you so long to look for me? I've been waiting for you.'

She'd been waiting for me? It was a kind of awakening. I hadn't considered that she'd been waiting for me.

It was the second time I'd heard her words and the first time I'd heard her voice. I seemed focused on the differences, and then I was surprised. Her voice didn't sound different. It sat within me. It was the voice that I would have heard before, it was the voice of the mother who created me, who carried me and who birthed me. Of course I'd heard her voice before. It sat within me. I was surprised that it was unsurprising. It just was.

As I rolled from side to side on the futon daybed, hanging onto every word, every sound, containing the pain in my gut and releasing a valve in my heart, I thankfully avoided a trip to the toilet. My head was spinning and my insides were emotionally and physically churning. It turned out I was a secret. A big secret. Her three other children didn't know about me. Her mother, sisters and brother didn't know about me. She needed some time to let them know. Her partner David knew. He'd known from the beginning. They met when she was pregnant. After I was born they moved to Melbourne and started their own family. They never married.

My eyes glistened with tears but there was no crying. There was intent listening and an intimacy I'd not known before. There was no blame, guilt or judgement. It just was. There was relief, sadness, loss and wonder. She stood in her hallway, away from her family to talk to me on the phone. When I realised the extent of her secret… that she'd kept it for 29 years, I imagined the personal toll that would take, and how it would have influenced other parts of her life. With her subsequent pregnancies and births, her parenting and the times throughout the years she encountered children who would have been my age.

'Did you have a happy life?' she wanted to know. I understood the enormity of that question. I'd known all about what happened to me, she did not. Anything could've happened. As I dreamed about the possibilities of my heritage, my belonging, she had also been dreaming of the possibilities. Relinquishing mothers, and society more generally, were all told at the time that 'it was the best decision for the child,' but it wasn't, not always. There were some horror stories, but not mine. Ann didn't know that, she knew nothing of me. Her knowledge of me lay between being buried in secrecy and denial and an ephemeral dream-state in the heavens. We can never know all the prayers, wishes and inner-most thoughts of others, even the ones we know and love best of all. I knew she had a relationship with god, I expect she would have prayed for me, and herself. It didn't seem my business to ask.

I reassured her that my life had been happy, but I felt like she wanted to hear the sugar-coated version. I wish I'd told her then how her absence was ever-present throughout my life. I wish I'd found the words to say much more but this was the first of many chances I'd get.

She asked me if I received any of the parcels she sent me. 'What parcels?' She had collected several baby items during her pregnancy which she had taken with her to the home for relinquishing mothers prior to giving birth and handed them over, with the understanding they would be going with me (her baby). In those early weeks and months, she sent several small parcels in the hope they were being sent on to me. As was the strict policy of the time, no personal items went with the baby and no contact, even through a third party, was possible between relinquishing mothers and their babies. She sounded hurt and disappointed when I told her I had nothing.

The day I arrived in Newcastle marked a new beginning for me and my new family, and Mum was determined to have nothing that could be attributed to the hospital, let alone my relinquishing mother, anywhere near her baby. There was considerable stigma tied up with the language used at the time, things like 'hussy', 'loose', 'without morals', 'she got herself into trouble', 'she brought shame to the family', 'we disowned her' – all painful and hurtful language. My adoption was initially delayed for one month due to ill health, and then I was made a Ward of the State for twelve months. My official adoption papers came through in 1966. Mum has always spoken about this with protective determination. I had a strong sense of her uneasiness during the time I was a Ward of the State, as there was a possibility I could be taken from her. She needed those adoption papers to ensure I belonged to her, to my family. Forever.

Ann and I were both desperate for photos of each other, and I told her I'd also send a poem I'd written on the day Mum first called her. Our phone call lasted over an hour, and when I hung up I rolled over with exhaustion, but also a newfound energy. I was fatigued and smiling. I'd found her! It was real! It went well. She wanted to know me! She'd not forgotten me. She'd always remembered. I was her first. I was a secret.

After recovering from that amazing phone call, I put together a couple of photos and the poem I'd written a few months earlier, on 8 March 1994, International Women's Day, and I posted it off to Ann. It was emotionally and symbolically monumental. I'm glad it was a photo first. It would give her time to sit with my image and some of my words, to realise the reality of her decision twenty-nine years ago. Thanks to the hundreds of photos taken on our world trip the year before, I had a few to choose from, but it was a huge decision. Hair up or hair down? What would the location say about me? Or what was I wearing? I didn't want one where I had sunglasses on. Then I found it. A smiling me in Hyde Park in London in front of a bed of red tulips, wearing a red top, black leather jacket and a silver Ankh symbol around my neck. I was extremely happy in that photo and in the wildest chance my life could be swayed or influenced by a greater force, I daresay the reason I wanted that photo taken of me that day was to have it to introduce myself to my birth mother. It really was perfect.

Photo I sent to Ann – her first sight of me, the daughter she gave up 29 years before

MY FIRST SIGHT

An envelope arrived soon after our first conversation. Ann had understood my plea to see her family; to understand where I came from. Who are my people? Would I recognise any of me in her? Tightly clutching the precious photo, I stared in silence, smiling. This was my first sight of my biological mother, standing with her siblings. This is where I came from. It had been their long-held tradition to be photographed whenever they were all together, in profile, in age order – oldest (Ann) on the right, down the line, Prudence, Barbara, Jimmy and Bronwyn. The photo could not have been more perfect. Their alikeness undeniable. My likeness absolutely recognisable in their eyes, smiles and dare I say, noses. I was immediately struck by their ages, so close to each other. I clung on to the photo for weeks, until every pixel was imprinted on my mind. I needed to recall it wherever I went, as my first tangible link, from where I came.

The phone rang.

'Hello, is that Karen?'

'Yes,' I reply.

'It's your aunty Bronwyn here!'

It was a brief first introduction to my beautiful aunt, brief because she was the only one in my family who lived in Melbourne and she was inviting me over to her place on Saturday afternoon. I couldn't quite believe it. Bursting with excitement, I felt sick with nerves.

Arriving in the quiet, wide street in Port Melbourne that day, I took a deep breath of a beautiful breeze and looked up at the clear blue sky. I parked easily out the front of her house. The front gate was wide open. The front door was also wide open. As I stepped onto the footpath I took a moment to contemplate and felt immediately welcome. This was before I'd seen anyone. I tapped the knocker on the open heavy wooden door and a beautiful silhouette of a woman came bouncing up the hallway with arms open. This is my aunt. We hugged for the longest time. It was the best hug of my life – where I felt no ending and no beginning, we were one. These were the arms, shoulder and heart of my kin, pressed against me for the first time in my life. As I held on, I looked over her shoulder to see another silhouette, of a smaller woman in the mid-distance. She was standing, smiling.

'Who's this?' I asked.

We released each other, and Bronwyn said, 'Karen, this is Nana.'

Oh, Nana! A beautiful smile, a magnificent head of snowy hair and the most engaged, glistening eyes of anyone I'd met. I was afraid my squeezing would break her on our first meeting – imagine if I killed Nana the first time we hugged! We sat and held hands, the three of us looking at each other in amazement. It was most joyous, yet sadness lingered in the knowledge we'd missed out on so much.

I found out that my amazing Nana had a wonderful lease on her new life after her children grew into their own adult lives. Her husband 'Old Jim' had died about twenty-five years earlier and in that time she'd moved to Melbourne to live in Elwood for a short stint. She'd lived in Lennox Head in northern New South Wales with her much-loved dog, a black Labrador called Ben, and had been on several trips abroad. The pride in her achievement of travelling to Nepal was obvious on their faces. I was so impressed that my Nana was so worldly, adventurous and clearly interested in learning. She had a present for me. She gave me a tiny jade Buddha that she brought back from Nepal. It remains one of my most precious treasures. I can't believe that my Nana gave me a Buddha – blowing away every perception I'd had about what a 'nana' was like.

Word was getting out. Ann had begun to tell her family. It was a great shock for Nana as it became evident that her husband, Ann's father, had known about Ann's pregnancy. He was the one who made all of the arrangements for the adoption. He sent Ann on a cruise to Fiji to recover from the birth. He decided what was best. He decided not to tell his wife that their daughter was pregnant, that she had a baby and that she relinquished her baby girl for adoption. Nana told me more than once, 'If only I'd known, she didn't have to give you away, I would've had you.'

Many families did – it wasn't uncommon for a baby born to an unmarried woman to be brought up as that woman's sibling. There are countless stories of women going to their grave with the secret that their little sister was actually their daughter – or that, close to death, a mother would reveal to her son that he is her grandson and that the woman he knew as his sister was the woman who gave birth to him. Explosive situations of the time, orchestrated 'in the interest of the child'. I'll never know how things would have turned out if Old Jim had told his wife about their daughter's pregnancy.

I've never once apportioned blame to my birth mother for my adoption. Perhaps it has something to do with the way Mum told me I was adopted. It was a positive story. She never outwardly indicated any ill will towards my birth mother or her character, although I did wonder in my teens if the overly strict and oppressive nature of my familial governance had any relation to the fact I was the daughter of an unmarried woman, a woman who had sex out of wedlock and therefore there was an ill-perceived risk the same thing could happen to me. I suspect it may have had something to do with the easily-won label of 'boy crazy'.

PIECE BY PIECE

Old Jim was many years older than his wife and quite worldly. With a university education, he was an accomplished pharmacist and small business owner. Nana described him as being devoted to his work, where he spent too much time, leaving her to look after their young family of five children. She told me he was 'difficult' and that she was very upset with him when he bought a third pharmacy in Newcastle without discussing it with her. It was meant to be a time to be enjoying some of the modest spoils afforded them, including family time at home and local holidays. Instead the third pharmacy meant Old Jim was busier than ever, working late nights and on weekends. As their children grew into their teens, the McGarry's home in Bar Beach was a haven for friends of the kids, although fewer adult friends and peers of Nana and Old Jim, possibly due to the scarcity of the time the couple had together.

In the early days of their courtship, Old Jim must have been a charmer. He was double the age of twenty-year-old Enid. They met when he had a pharmacy in Bathurst and Enid was working as a domestic for a local family. One of her daily tasks was visiting the pharmacy for medication for someone in the family who was in poor health, and it was during these visits she got to know Jim. He was an authoritarian figure from the get-go, both towards Nana's younger sister (who hated him for it) and, I gather to a lesser degree, the woman he was to marry.

One of the huge revelations after connecting with Ann was that we went to the same high school. I wish I could have known that when I was there. I wonder how that might have shaped my experience? I realise those sorts of wishes are pointless, but it gave me great comfort to know that for a time, I walked in her footsteps. Literally. We would have walked up the steps to the quadrangle, up the driveway entrance to the school, we would have crossed the road to attend chapel and, countless times, we would have both walked up the steps to Newcastle Cathedral for weekly services and other significant events. I often felt peace in that cathedral; I also felt power and awe. I watched while others clamoured to be close to the hierarchy, but for me it was the acoustics, the art and the ceremony. The occasions when the cathedral choir was in residence were magical. Ann sang in the choir.

Of course, I'd walked in the footsteps of my mum and dad, my big brothers, my Mumma and Poppa, Nanna and Pop. I loved them and would follow them everywhere; I cried when I was stopped with a command to 'stay there' or 'you can't come here'. It usually had to do with my age, or stage, or ill-perceived judgement of my ability to understand. There were movies I couldn't watch, shows I couldn't go to – I was devastated to miss *Jesus Christ Superstar* – and funerals were a big no-no. I missed the funerals of my Pop and Poppa and my baby nephew Justin. This was my family I'd grown up with, the family whose folklore I imbibed as my own, but every now and then there was a pushback, back into my place. The reasons for the pushback are varied – gender – definitely, age – to an extent, birth order, yes, and what I mainly perceived as the generation gap. Have I mentioned that my parents brought me up in the 70s like they were bringing me up in the 50s? One of my favourite TV shows was *Happy Days*, and my friends and I would often comment and joke how I was living the life of Joanie Cunningham, my Mum was Marion and Dad was Howard. I was living in a time warp so any wonder I couldn't sleep for a week after I actually did get to see the Time Warp in the *Rocky Horror Picture Show* – around the time Meatloaf's 'Bat out of Hell' came out.

THE SYDNEY YEARS

One of the names on the pieces of paper Ann sent me with that first photo was that of her school friend, Julie. They'd been best friends at Newcastle Grammar and both of them gained entry to university in Sydney. Ann was following in her father's footsteps, studying pharmacology – Julie studied medicine. It was the early 60s and the prospect of young women leaving regional areas to study at university in Sydney was not common. Given my own upbringing I'm still blown away at Ann's and Julie's opportunities, given they happened five decades before I saw it as a possibility for myself. What these young women had in opportunity they also had in responsibility, obligation and a life governed and monitored by their parents, the university, their chaperones and the state. The out-of-towners like Ann and Julie were housed in boarding houses with many rules, especially concerning visitors and curfews. Studies were a priority and incorporating part-time work was a necessity for Ann.

There was still time for socialising, and by all accounts, Ann was fun to be around. She was intelligent, witty and gregarious. Ann and Julie found their way into the Italian supper-club scene of Sydney in the early to mid-60s. They met lots of people and made many friends, especially with the musicians in a band. The well-dressed, good-looking Italian men with exotic accents enjoyed their time on the weekends, when they could play music, dance and meet up with friendly Australians more or less on their own terms, leaving the week of hard manual labour and any homesickness behind them. They had their music and firm bonds with each other. Like so many migrants with shared experiences, they stuck together and supported each other.

In 1963 Julie married Gionni and Ann was her bridesmaid. Gionni managed The Swiss, a restaurant in Lane Cove, and for a time the young couple lived above it with their small children. Julie completed her studies and became a doctor. On several occasions Ann invited her Italian friends and their Aussie girlfriends to Newcastle on weekend visits, where they met the rest of the family at the Bar Beach home. Ann told me she was really keen on a bloke named Frank, but things didn't work out and she 'ended up with the wrong guy'.

In May 1964, Ann became pregnant. At the time she was studying, and working part-time at the cosmetics counter at David Jones. I was amazed she was a DJs shop assistant, the likes of whom I was fascinated by as a child. Due to the invasive shadowing by Matron and the chaperones at the Business Girls Hostel in Commonwealth Street in Sydney, Ann needed to find accommodation on her own terms and moved into an independent boarding house in Rose Bay. She maintained her job for a time, and kept in and contact with her family and friends by phone calls or letters. For a while her friends didn't notice anything unusual, she hid her pregnancy well.

Thankfully Ann wasn't completely alone. Soon after moving into the new boarding house in Rose Bay, she met two English lads, brothers named Bob and David. They'd just arrived from England and shared a room at the end of the hallway.

Ann and David became great friends and confidantes, becoming closer as her pregnancy developed. It must have been a stressful, confusing and isolating time for Ann – to have feelings for David reciprocated, at a time when her father was making arrangements for her to give up her baby. David assured Ann that adoption wasn't the only option and he offered to assume the fatherhood of the baby. Whether or not this was a proposal of marriage is not certain, but it matters not, as Ann firmly told David that it was neither his problem nor his business; her decision was made and she would be doing things her way. How much in fact it was 'her way' is unclear as her father, Old Jim, stepped in to make all the necessary arrangements.

Ann told her story directly to me, with no fluff and no space for emotion or curiosity. She held a strong gaze and just told it. For many years I explained her manner as being a result of having kept her pregnancy and my birth a secret for so long, for having gone through a life-changing and life-giving event, basically alone. She was very matter-of-fact, to the point of being blunt. That was her way.

Late in her pregnancy, a bunch of Ann's friends, including Julie and Gionni, came to visit Ann at her new boarding house. They discovered Ann was pregnant by looking at her, and assumed that David and Ann were having a baby together. At some stage Ann had confided the name of the baby's father to Julie, and told her of the impending adoption. This man and his girlfriend were among the visitors that day, and Ann told me that she took a private moment to tell him he was the father.

'How much money do you want me to give you?' he asked.

'I want nothing from you,' she replied. She didn't see him again.

About a month before my birth, Ann was sent to a home for relinquishing mothers, to receive the antenatal care she needed. I suspect such a place aided unmarried mothers to keep a low profile, as it brought untold shame on families and society in general. I suspect such a place would have kept these unmarried pregnant women in a state of compliance, where boyfriends or family members could hold no sway over their final decision. Such a place would have kept these unmarried pregnant women in 'safe hands', ready to deliver healthy babies into the arms of good, Christian, married couples who desperately wanted to give a baby a home and moral upbringing, 'in the best interest of the child'. The unmarried pregnant women would have been kept in a state of compliance for legal authority, to surrender all parental rights, identification and potential for contact. My heart aches for the position these women and girls were in. This particular time was on the cusp of the sexual revolution, the advent of birth control in the hands of women and soon after, the gradual acceptance of single motherhood and social security with the introduction of the single-mother's pension. My heart continues to ache for those women, the unwanted women in our society, the women whose appearance and presence was too disturbing for everyone else, for families, for landlords, for employers, for the church and parishioners and for the government. My heart continues to ache for the children of those women who were robbed of their identity and their truth.

There were women who willingly and openly chose to give up their babies without any coercion at all. Ann may have been one of them. I support any woman to have agency over their decisions, particularly regarding their own fertility. However, it's hard to be confident that all women in Ann's situation in 1965 had complete power in their decisions. It is most likely their decisions were informed by the widespread attitude that their existence was a blighted stain on the social psyche, and having a child out of wedlock would have made housing, employment, education and future relationships near impossible. The stigma for both mother and child would have endured for the bulk of their lives, and I believe this is the reason why decisions to relinquish babies and adopt babies were considered to be 'in the best interest of the child'.

Like many relinquishing mothers, Ann didn't see me after I was born. All she knew was she gave birth to a baby girl. She had to live for over two decades not knowing if I lived or died. What hell that must have been. My empathy for Ann, for what it's worth, is born from my own self, my own experiences and values and core beliefs. I wonder where empathy and ego intersect and how we can genuinely empathise with another. From everything she projected, Ann was clear on her decisions and her rationale and didn't feel the need or responsibility to explain it to anyone. I empathised with her every step of the way. I needed to fill in the cracks with love, reasoning and truth, which is how I came to find her, to discover my family and to fall in love and be loved and accepted by my kin.

I AM THE REVELATION

The unexpected news of my existence landed on top of my half-siblings like a forty-foot wave they didn't see coming. In the midst of a family upheaval of their own, Ann, without saying a word, placed my first correspondence to her in the middle of the kitchen table. My photo sat on top of the pile in plain view.

'What does Bronwyn have to do with any of this?' one of her children questioned. 'It's not Bronwyn. Look closely,' Ann replied.

It soon became evident the photos were not of their aunt. The woman in the photo was their sister. Me.

One of my half-siblings sat in stunned silence, one rushed out the back door sobbing, and one retreated to their room. The natural order of the family had been disrupted. The known and imagined history of their mother, disrupted. She never lied to them, but she successfully omitted a significant part of her story, for reasons only known to her. It was only eight years prior when she wrote the letter of enquiry regarding my survival. At that point, twenty-one years after giving birth, she didn't know if I lived or died. When would have been the right time to have the conversation with her children? What could she say?

I can't speak for the feelings experienced by my half-siblings – only from the way they responded towards me. I felt completely loved and accepted by one, and a spectrum from ambivalence to suspicion by the others. I walked into their lives with cautious optimism, excitedly trying to manage my expectations. To have a brother and sisters who were of my generation, my age group, peers with whom I could share cultural references – our loves, likes and desires, whom we could learn from, joke and laugh with, recognising ourselves in each other. I dared not include brothers and sisters in my dreaming all these years – it seemed too risky and open to disappointment.

PIECES BY PIECES

Andrew and I had planned a trip to Sydney, and we arranged to meet Julie and Gionni. We were met with open arms and smiles and such a wonderful sense of enthusiasm, love and curiosity. As I sat in their lounge room in their suburban home in Sydney's north, I felt excited and somewhat bewildered at the ease in which we responded to each other's questions. Their daughter Joanna was also there, and she recalled how much she loved being with Ann as a child. She felt they had a special relationship and wondered aloud if it might have had something to do with Ann tracking me, the daughter she'd given up, through Joanna, who is of a similar age. 'Every 8th of February, on your birthday, I would think of you,' Julie told me. 'Whenever I had a patient the same age I would wonder if it could be you, Ann's baby.'

I was overwhelmed at the thought of having a fairy-like godmother throughout my whole life. The realisation I had someone in the world I didn't know, yet who knew, remembered and cared about me, filled my soul with love and sadness simultaneously. I had no idea what I'd find when I lifted the lid of the mystery box of my story. That day I heard the tinkling sounds reminiscent of a music-box ballerina swirling around in my mind.

As I listened and talked some more, highly animated with excitement, I became aware of the way the three of them looked at me. They'd give each other knowing glances and look some more. I became a little self-conscious. Eventually they remarked how much I was like Ann. They couldn't believe the way I spoke and particularly my gestures were so similar to Ann's. They recognised Ann in me. I couldn't believe it either! How could this be? I hadn't even met Ann yet. Could this be what it is known as nature versus nurture? I loved hearing them compare me to Ann. It was an early affirmation of my belonging. I continued talking and listening, with an assured confidence that I had another history, another place where I belonged.

Julie showed me her wedding album, which contained many photos of Ann as their bridesmaid, a year or so before I was born. These photos were from a time when Ann was a young, attractive single woman who had the world at her feet. She was living, loving and laughing in Sydney, determined to complete her studies. This was my first sight of the young woman who would soon become pregnant with me. She looked absolutely beautiful. I was stunned. I wish I'd had the chance to pore over those photos all day, all by myself. I could have stared at these photos for hours, instead, in the presence of strangers, trying to absorb every word, expression and piece of information, committing it to my memory, I was overwhelmed and worried I'd miss something. This is the woman who attracted the man who would become my father. As all of this was going through my mind, Julie asked, 'Karen, do you know who your father is?'

'No, we didn't get that far in our phone call, but I will be asking as soon as I get the chance.'

For the time being I was grateful to find out what I could about Ann and her family. Julie and Gionni looked at each other and Julie said, 'We know who he is.'

'Really?' I replied, smiling. They explained they were not in contact with him anymore but had seen him a few months previously, at the funeral of one of their friend's parents.

'He lives not far from here.'

Again, another box presented itself, should I choose to open it. Julie was insistent, 'If Ann hasn't told you, well, it's not our place to say.'

I agreed. Absolutely. I had no hesitation. This was enough information for now, and if Julie and Gionni knew who he was, that indicated strongly to me that Ann would tell me and I'd wait until we actually met face-to-face.

I was baffled why Ann and Julie had lost contact, yet Ann had wanted us to meet. So my wonderful afternoon with Julie, Gionni, Joanna and Andrew wound down and I bounced down their driveway with a head full of information and questions, but mostly an exploding heart.

∞

I'VE ALWAYS, ALWAYS LOVED having birthdays. Ever since I can remember I was excited to the point of sleeplessness several nights before my actual day. I didn't have many parties, so it wasn't the party as such. And I felt so awkward and overwhelmed with people singing *Happy Birthday* to me that I'd bury my head somewhere to hide from the attention. I did love the cake and the candles, the ritual of darkening the room in readiness for the lit beacons atop a modestly decorated cake – the moments anticipating the candles and the song were exhilarating. Of course, I loved the presents but they weren't a guaranteed thrill like the cake. Every one of my birthdays I put a thought out there to my birth mother, whoever and wherever she was, thanking her for choosing to have me and for making the decision to give me away. I'd found a wonderful loving family and I was happy. I hoped, and for a long time prayed, that she was ok and that she remembered me on my birthday and that it didn't make her sad. As I got older I realised even more how there may have been another option for her. She could've decided to terminate her pregnancy, and I was grateful for the decision she made. The ripple effect of that decision was profound. For good, for great and for bad.

On my thirtieth birthday I arranged to meet friends for dinner at a favourite Mexican restaurant in Swan Street, Richmond. It was the precursor to a big party I'd planned for Saturday night. A dozen of us were talking and laughing over cocktails while checking out the menu. Then a surprise delivery arrived – the hugest bunch of gerberas I'd ever seen in the brightest and sunniest of colours. Bronwyn, my newfound aunty, dropped into the restaurant and gave me a huge hug to wish me happy birthday. It was the first birthday since she'd known about me and the first birthday I'd known from where I came. And from whom. I briefly pondered what we'd missed and how I valued and celebrated birthdays. She remembered, she cared, she listened and she showed up. She expected nothing. She came and went and left my heart soaring and smile beaming. I adored my birthday.

Over the coming months there were more trips from Melbourne to Newcastle. Every trip home since finding Ann I would drive up and down Wrightson Avenue in Bar Beach, trying to put my finger on my connection with this place. My recurring flying dreams of my childhood took place over these rooftops and cliff tops, swooping up and down the landscape, along streets and hovering over backyards. The year I spent just about every weekend and school holidays visiting Tim in that same street, lying in his driveway watching him restore his car. Hanging out at his mate's place next door, and the big party at the house across the road. Three houses in that street I frequented at a time when I had no idea that a few doors up sat the place where my mother lived with her parents, her sisters and brother. I was treading in their footsteps without having a clue. I was connected to this place without understanding why. Somehow it had been imprinted in my psyche.

THE BIG DAY

In the wee hours of our tenth anniversary, Andrew surprised me with an unexpected wedding proposal he'd been working on for weeks. He was, and still is, the man of my dreams and I leapt into his arms, squealing a resounding 'Yes!' We announced our engagement on 9 September 1995 and hoped for a wedding in our favourite season – autumn. The word of our news started to spread and was met with much excitement from our families and friends.

Shortly afterwards I started receiving phone calls from people I'd never met.

'Hello is that Karen?'

'Yes, it is.'

'Hello Karen, this is your aunty from Adelaide. I hear you're getting married.'

'Hello is that Karen?'

'Yes, it is, who is this?'

'Hello Karen, this is your aunty from Maitland [Hunter Valley, NSW]. Can we come to your wedding?'

Two aunties had called me, the ones from the photo. I'd already met Bronwyn and Nana but now… more family excited to meet me after hearing about the wedding. We decided to invite Ann, Nana, the aunties and my uncle to the wedding. It wasn't for another five months so I thought Ann and I would be meeting at some point before then. We didn't.

I needed to see Nana again so we arranged a visit at her unit in East Maitland. It was wonderful. We sat and had a cup of tea and talked some more. My uncle Jimmy was on his way over and another aunt, Prudence, was popping in after work. Prudence's reputation of being the family chatterbox preceded her, so the irony that she had laryngitis at the time she was to meet the biggest secret and newest family member wasn't lost on anyone. Nana and Jimmy thought it was hilarious and knew it would kill Prudence not being able to speak to me. She arrived with much excitement, and what she lacked in volume and articulation she made up for in smiles, hugs and expression.

We sat around for a bit longer and we talked about what had happened and how I still hadn't met Ann – I was fuelled by our phone call and the photos. I can't remember why neither of us just jumped on a plane to go and meet. It was a bit like an old-fashioned courtship, and she was allowing everyone the time to get on board with everything. It didn't bother me too much at the time, I was going with the flow and every week there seemed to be an unfolding of information – or that the lid of that music box was opening wider to release more of the song.

I asked more questions of everyone, trying to picture their lives and where they'd come from. I'd always ask about Old Jim but the information didn't always flow so easily.

'Isn't it interesting that Ann and David never married?' I asked.

'What?' Everybody responded with a stony silence and gaping jaws.

I had no idea I was making a surprise revelation. How could the family not know that Ann and David were never married?

'Did you go to a wedding?' I queried.

It seemed nobody went to a wedding or heard about a wedding however they all assumed Ann and David were married and were very surprised to hear they weren't. Then Nana said for the second time, tellingly as she shrugged and shook her head and said, 'Nothing Ann does surprises me.'

And so it was. More stories, more sharing and more wonder.

The family resemblance was astounding. Having grown up as a physical outsider, resembling nobody, the recognition and familiarity impacted on my inward and outward being. I started to look at myself differently as I now had a vision that fitted me. I could now see forward and where I was going. My guess is that most people who grow up with their biological family take it for granted. Sure, some people are turned off by it – especially in abusive and neglectful families. I get that. Biological familiarity is the assumed norm and like every other norm, when you don't fit in, you feel left out. I'd always felt different and tried my best to work it to my advantage. Freedom to express the way I physically appeared to myself and others was important. I had no template. I was a blank slate. I could be anyone. Once I started to reconcile the fact I had Italian heritage it gave a home to my nose. I had to learn to embrace it. However, the nose could have been a red herring, like completely on the nose! The nose was from Ann's side of the family. There was the McGarry nose, but then again, I reckon Nana had it too, so maybe it was the nose from the maternal line. I don't nose!

As Julie and Gionni pointed out that day in Lane Cove, the physical resemblance was strong. I felt it. And it gave me peace and a sense of belonging. I started to wonder… if I have all this physical resemblance with the McGarrys, what part of me is from my father? This question has remained constant for over twenty years.

∞

ANN'S FLIGHT WAS DUE to arrive in Melbourne the night before my wedding. I really didn't want my first meeting with my birth mother to be at my wedding, so I arranged with Bronwyn to pick Ann up at the airport. Andrew and I arrived at Bronwyn's in the afternoon where we met my aunties and uncle, and Nana of course – all of whom were buzzing at the excitement of Ann and I finally meeting. I went along with the suggestion from one of the aunties that they all come to the airport to witness their older sister meet her daughter for the first time. Bron and I drove in her car and another carload with the aunts and uncle travelled separately. Andrew understood I needed that moment alone with my family and he waited at Bron's place with some others. Off we went. The night before my wedding. To the airport. To meet my birth mother.

We arrived at the gate after a tense, excited and tentative walk from the car, and waited for the flight from Launceston to land. Keeping watch on the terminal monitors was excruciating. Flight landed. Disembarking had commenced. Sliding doors at the arrival gate opened and closed before and after each grouping of passengers arrived. Standing ten metres from the doors, I waited, barely breathing. The doors opened, I inhaled deeply. Is that her? No. Is that her? No. Deep exhale. Doors closed. The doors opened again, I inhaled deeply. Is that her? No, that's not her. Where is she? Is that her? No. Doors closed. Deep exhale. We waited some more. Those doors open and closed letting through small groups of people, about six more times. The doors opened. She was unmistakable. Her salt and pepper coloured hair was long and wild. She was smiling and coming straight for me. She came to me. I stood there and she came. Our hug was hard. She squeezed me so tightly it hurt. We were matched in height which made that first physical connection easy. I knew the others were watching and tearing up. They knew the enormity of the moment for their sister and imagined what it might have been like for me. We walked to the bar, my head whirring almost out of control. I tried to savour every moment speeding around me. Somebody ordered sparkling wines and we stood there, flushed with excitement and emotion, staring, smiling and with tears in our eyes. As we made our way to the car park I heard Ann exclaim behind me, 'You have no bum, just like me!' It was a remark without inhibition, a familial remark where she recognised herself in me. I felt unequivocally part of something, someone.

THE BIG DAY

The others went in one direction to their car, Bron, Ann and I headed to ours and I was super keen to get back to Bron's to meet up with Andrew, Nana and the rest. Placing Ann's luggage in the boot, we hopped in the car ready to leave. The car wouldn't start. It *couldn't* start. We weren't going anywhere. The others had left and we were in the car park. Bron walked back to the terminal to call for roadside assistance while Ann and I stood there… waiting… practicing our small talk… wondering what the hell was going to happen. We had time in each other's presence, within an hour of meeting for the first time, on the gravely ground at Melbourne Airport car park, the night before my wedding. We waited for Bron to return, then we waited some more. It was after 9pm we finally made it back to Bron's house in Albert Park. Everyone was really worried. We should've been back almost two hours ago and poor Andrew was sitting in the lounge room surrounded by a bunch of people he hardly knew, waiting for me to return from a momentous meeting. It was precious relief when we saw each other. The house was buzzing as we shared food and a drink in the courtyard, everybody speaking at once, trying to absorb and process the evening's event.

For many reasons our wedding day was the best day of my life. I smiled and glowed all day long, propelled by my love for my Andrew. In addition, it was the first time my family had met his family, although our parents had met each other several times in our ten years together, they hadn't met our siblings – all of whom were just names in stories recounted when updating on whereabouts and births of grandchildren.

Our families were uniting around us. More than that, my birth mother, her siblings and her mother were witnessing me among my people and meeting the family who loved me and grew me. They would gain insight into what they'd missed. This was the day, our wedding day, when Mum and Ann met for the first time. Sometime prior to my arrival, among the circle of gum trees on the banks of the Yarra River, they caught each other's eyes for the first time. I was with my 'best woman' Georgina getting ready for my big day and missed the moment of their introduction. I wondered about their body language, their embrace, their expressions and words. What did Dad say? How did they really feel? It was their daughter's wedding day.
Our wedding was a class act. Andrew and our best man Frank waited for us in the circle of gum trees by the bank of the Yarra River. The 1958 Hudson pulled up at the curb and when Dad opened the door I burst forth, beaming with love and anticipation and looking a million bucks. I couldn't wait!

My dear friend's dad bag-piped us down the hill, towards our people waiting there, towards the man I'd chosen to spend my life with, the man I wanted to grow old with and make many decisions with – to evolve into the best people possible. Ann and Nana, with my aunties and an uncle, were seated up front. They had an unobstructed view into my being and the love I had with Andrew. They could tell from where they were sitting that we were loved by our families and friends, all of whom were there to share our day.

As I stood before my people on that day, expressing my love and commitment to Andrew, the enormity of such an occasion that brought our families and friends together for the first time, was not lost. My brothers hadn't met any of my friends, and most of my friends had never met my parents or the rest of my family. I will never forget the sentiments expressed by Georgina, in her outstanding best-woman speech which spoke of families. She spoke about the coming together of three families and the profundity of the occasion. Apart from my stunning gold satin and lace dress, and the best-looking bridal party ever, the first appearance of my biological family was something that separated this wedding from any other.

Second only to the time when Andrew and I fell deeply in love and started our life together, I felt a strong sense of completion. My biological mystery had been resolved and declared in public, everyone was smiling and welcoming and willing. The energy and love was palpable. It was another arrival.

THE GLASS BOWL – PART 1

It was the happiest day of my life, my entire being beamed happiness and love. I felt completely supported and celebrated on the day I married my love and the day my families came together for the very first time.

Ann beamed back at me. I interpreted her beams as love and pride. Her hand brimming with rose petals, she extended her arm out and up and showered me with her love. It was

Ann showering me with petals on my wedding day, the day after we first met

a moment in time which I wanted to freeze and capture and put it in my locket. We had so much to catch up on, time to make up, stories to tell and ultimately be present, to be *in each other's presence*. I've reflected on the photograph that captured this moment. Ann's face is visible as I face her, my back to the camera.

I imagined each petal she showered on me carried a word, a wish, a hope – in celebration of where we'd come from and where we were going. They left her clutches with the best intentions and such positivity.

Family
Belonging
Homecoming
Recognition
Connection
Arrival
Ancestors
Acknowledgement
Gratitude
Pride
Love

I scooped up the petals and lovingly placed them in the hand-crafted rose-coloured glass bowl Ann had gifted us for our wedding. It was the first gift from my birth mother. I have kept it in pride-of-place in our three homes over many years.

SISTERS

Finding out I had sisters filled an ever-present gaping hole throughout my life. I'd desperately wanted a sister. It's strange to miss something I'd never had. Whenever my friends would talk about their sisters I'd feel a tiny bubble pop inside of me. It wasn't distressing, but I felt every pop every time. I still do. Maybe that's why I attempted to make my own sisters over the years, through friendships. I was happy to place this news at a treasured distance.

From what I'd observed and understood through first and second-hand accounts, the relationship with my sister Jacinta – the one who had always believed herself to be the oldest child – never took off. How much she felt jilted from that pole position or betrayed because of the secret I was, I'll never know. Maybe she didn't like me. I approached her with a ready and open heart, but we didn't fly. I let it be. My other sister, Madeline, and I began to fall in love, a love which was reciprocated in equal measure. In the early stages of love, my heart extends to the stratosphere, beyond the reach of mortals. The higher you love the harder you fall. I hear it. I feel it. I've felt it.

We fell for each other.

Our first meeting seemed to take forever. We had exchanged a few carefully worded letters before I managed to get to Sydney to arrange a visit. Walking up a dusty inner-city street one windy afternoon, the swirling leaves and filth from the road mirrored the feeling inside my head. My heart beat faster, my breathing became shallow, and I know this because I can feel it all over again as I recall the day, the day I was meeting my sister. I knocked on the door and waited. I knocked again and waited some more. I knocked again. No answer. I left a note under the enormous solid wooden door of the double story brick terrace that was crammed on the side of that busy street and with disbelief and disappointment, I walked away. Something had gone terribly wrong. I knew she wanted to meet me and was 95 per cent confident that she wasn't avoiding me. There was no phone, no other way to contact her other than by mail. I had to leave without knowing. I didn't know when I'd be back.

Days after returning home, I found out by mail the sad and frustrating news that she had sat at home in her room that day waiting for me and I never arrived! She did get my note sometime after but hadn't heard my feeble, tentative knock on the enormous solid wooden door of her two-story brick terrace on a busy road. She hadn't heard me! So we were to wait for our time.

It was October 1996 and I was in Sydney for the ARIA Awards as a couple of Smartartists stable mates had been nominated for some big gongs. Madeline and I arranged to meet on a busy Paddington corner. What did she look like? Would I recognise her? I got out of my taxi and crossed at the lights, looking intently at everyone. A woman slouched, leaning against a wall; her head was down and her dark, silky, wavy hair hung low. As I hurried toward her while maintaining a cool, confident and considered exterior, yet broadly beaming, she looked up. There she was. We hugged excitedly and she led me to an empty cafe where we sat and talked for nearly three hours. Just like a first date, we only had eyes for each other. We talked incessantly, asked questions, ordered coffee, juice, coffee, a toastie that was left uneaten. She went to the bathroom and I noticed we weren't alone. There was a man sitting at a nearby table. He had a computer and he was frenetically typing. We spoke about him and wondered in whispers if he could hear our conversation and what a fucking great conversation ours would be to listen in on. Two women – sisters, meeting for the first time in their lives and falling for each other. We joked that he could be writing a novel and we'd turn up as characters of his bestseller in ten years' time.

Over the coming months we wrote to each other with passionate regularity. Her letters to me were handwritten with romantic styling etched, inked, scratched and blotted on re-purposed paper, her rejected artwork or duplicate prints, anything she could find. A lot on brown paper, almost all of them sealed with wax. She was so clever and artistically gifted. She had the benefit of growing up with books and being an avid reader and student. University was where she felt she belonged. A thinker and a creator not suited for the contemporary world. She often remarked that she was born in the wrong time.

My letters to her by contrast were typed on white paper. No matter what I did I couldn't make them organic or spontaneous like hers. It's not that I edited my letter-writing, I'm an excellent typist and used to pride myself on the fact that I could type faster than I could think. The typeface template I chose couldn't compete with her handwriting, and no font could provide details about me. Her letters were filled with our mutual love and her love and passion for her boyfriend, music, literature, art and Elvis! Yes! Elvis! We both idolised The King! This was one of the most wonderful affirming surprises. Neither of us shared our infatuation with anyone else in our families growing up.

Madeline and I became each other's biggest fans. I adored her and couldn't help but stare at her whenever we met. I pored over her letters, reading them silently, then aloud and then silently again. I'd hold on to them as if it were bringing me closer to my long-lost sister, the sister I never knew I had, the sister who longed for me without knowing I existed, the sister who was excited and grateful to have me in her life. This woman, who was creative, intelligent, beautiful and curious, was my sister. She visited Melbourne just before Christmas in 1996 and stayed with us in Windsor for a couple of nights. We got to know each other better, still in disbelief at the unfolding of events. Our endless conversations covered all kinds of subjects; families, our childhoods, our passions, music – particularly The Fauves, Smashing Pumpkins, Elvis – education, travel, history, England, art, literature and on and on and on we went. It was bliss.

LIFTING THE LID

With every week a new piece of my life's puzzle emerged or was put into place. Some time after the wedding, Ann came back to Melbourne and we arranged to spend some important time together, getting to know one another. She was staying in Rye with Bron and her family, and invited Andrew and I down to visit for the day. The power and perspective of memory is curious – giving technicolour and surround-sound treatment in selecting the stories that I believe mean the most. As memories become embedded into the psyche, with each telling we recount those that make great stories, which resonate with their unique vibration, and in my case, revelation. After sharing a beautiful meal, the first prepared and shared with my kin, we enjoyed a walk to watch the waves crashing on the shore, but the finale came after dinner when everyone left Ann and I to talk at the dining table.

Over the past few years, without much forethought, I'd hastily stored my small collection of paperwork and correspondence relating to the history of my adoption in a tan cardboard ring-hole folder, covered in a random placement of found stickers and doodling. Without inhibition I brought the scrappy folder with me to Rye and as we sat together and talked, I showed Ann the contents. It was difficult to fully gauge her response. Some things she looked at for a long time, others she flipped through. There were documents completed around the time of my birth by social workers – an attempt to piece together some information on my parentage and Ann's character. She had just turned twenty-one at the time of my birth. In 1964 it would have been more common for women of that age to be in a steady relationship and heading for a matrimonial future. Women seeking alternative fulfilment by actively participating in education, employment and the wave of social change that was beginning to sweep the western world would have been a slowly growing minority.

My understanding and empathy for women of that era in Australia runs deeper than some, perhaps because I was a relinquished baby. Conservative societal attitudes were informed and influenced by Christianity, which enjoyed such fervent dominance over the public and private lives of Australian citizens.

So we flipped through the pages in the folder. There were descriptions of Ann as a young woman as 'very attractive' and a 'fine type of girl' who was interested in music and played the piano. The information about my father? Ah yes… the father whom I knew to be of Italian descent and nothing else. Some of the records described him as being a tailor or tracer by trade, of being 26 years old, of having six siblings. One said he played guitar. They described his height and eye colour. Presumably, informed by interviewing Ann. As she flipped through the pages of details in the handwriting of a social worker or typed words on a page by a hospital clerk, she commented with grunts and the occasional 'Well that's not true' and 'Or that.'

I don't know why I didn't hold her to those comments at the time and ask her exactly which pieces of information she disputed. There was a lot to take in, for both of us. I was busy watching her face, her expressions and eyes, her hands and shapes of her fingers, listening to the tone of her voice. I was trying to absorb everything, knowing I'd be missing vital clues.

I showed her the card that was tied to my wrist when, as a one-month-old baby, the nurse delivered me to the stationmaster at Broadmeadow railway station. 'Baby McGarry'. She stared long and hard at several of the items. Our conversation went from free flowing to stagnant. I wish I could replay every detail over again in my mind.

Then she asked me: 'Do you have any questions?'

Of course I had one really big question.

'Who is my father?'

There came the stare, the longest deepest look into my eyes and beyond. She must have been expecting me to ask. It's a question that anyone in my situation would want answered. It's a question I'm constantly asked by friends, new and old.

'Silvio Nino.' She replied.

I had a name. It was gold to me.

'Do not go and find him,' she continued. 'He had a girlfriend at the time and they went on to marry. They had a son, named Anthony. It was complicated.'

The Folder

Flipping and unfolding the pages of my file
The story of my being emerges
Records, reports, certificates and observations
By people whom I'd never know

Scraping together the pieces of the puzzle
When the edges are torn and jagged
Results in imperfection and gaps
Overlapping recollections

When pen takes to paper at the hand of a stranger
There is more substance to its content and intent
When words are read aloud the current is stronger
These waters run deeper to build and affirm memories

The folder began as an envelope in the back of a wardrobe
It's growth due to time, courage, curiosity and need
Now in order to create a stronger picture
The letters, forms, doodles and questions
(Many answers, more questions)

My point of reference which became my point of difference
To which I'd occasionally return
Most of it etched beneath my skin
Re-telling to friends and strangers, who then became friends
Brought me strength, direction and ease

I showed her the folder, she flipped through the pages
I couldn't be sure which lines she was reading or overlooking
'That's not true,' 'they got that wrong'
But look at everything they got right

'Do you have any questions?' she asked
'Who is my father?'
The deepest stare into my soul, held for a time
Awkward silence
She gave his name with a warning

It was complicated, he had a girlfriend at the time,
They went on to be married and had a son
I showed him my pregnant belly and he offered me money
To go away
I'd make my own decisions and I rejected his money

For years I heeded her warning
Until my need became greater than her threat
It grew inside my heart and mind every day
My story needed completing
I'd make my own decision and I'd do it without her

HOMECOMING

Andrew and I were planning a visit to Tasmania in January 1997, a few weeks after we'd spent those days with Madeline, with a plan to meet the rest of the family and take some time to road trip around a place that had been calling us for years. We flew from Melbourne to Devonport and hired a car to drive around the island. Our first stop was Launceston where Ann and David and their kids (my 'half' sisters and brother) were expecting us. There was definitely an expectant feeling in the air as we drove south towards Launceston. The world felt, looked and sounded different. I was a participant as well as a spectator.

We took little notice of the storm clouds following us and were relieved to have found our way around a new city and to our destination. We pulled up outside Ann's house. Sitting in the car we looked up in awe. Before us on a steep grassy hill we were overshadowed by the tallest pine trees, standing in strength in front of a beautiful, historic two-storey house, the house and trees on the hill. As I stared absorbing the enormity of the moment, contemplating what might have been and making comparisons to what I'd known, it was like staring at the Addams Family House. With that thought a huge thunderclap jolted me into the present moment. Together we gasped.

'Whoa!' Andrew said.

'Is this an omen?' I replied.

In determined solidarity, Andrew and I ducked out of the car to the sound of another thunderclap, a lightning bolt and heavy, heavy rain. Heads down shielding from the storm we ran up the side path and were suddenly met by a man with the kindest eyes. It was David, the man who, had Ann made different choices, could have been a father to me.

I was about to dive into the arms and surrounds of a family that could have been mine. In many ways it was mine. More than photos and words on a page this would be total immersion where I would walk, smell and breathe in the rooms of the home that could have formed me. With my people. Apart from the house on the hill, the trees, thunder, lightning and downpour, the man with the kind eyes welcomed me through the back door of the family home. On the kitchen table sat the hugest wheel of cheese I'd ever seen! My favourite, camembert.

This was the first meeting of my other siblings. It was a new world for me. I'd always been the youngest, by miles. Growing up my age made me feel equally special and excluded. In this family I was facing a level playing field and felt out of my depth. I desperately wanted genuine interaction. I was wise enough to know meaningful connection would happen with time, if at all. I was coming into their home, their lives, for which they were unprepared; they certainly didn't ask for this. I might have been a novelty at best, an intrusion at worst.

My way of absorbing the information through my senses and my collective being was to observe and respond. I hope they appreciated my attempts to authentically reach them.

I was becoming more comfortable in this strange, new familiarity.

'What would you like to do for dinner?' Ann asked. 'We could go out or I can cook anything you would like.'

I took a moment to consider her offering and how I felt, what I needed.

'Could we have a family dinner at home?' I asked.

My wish granted, we sat down to a roast dinner at home around the dining table, and Ann offered to make chocolate pudding for dessert. The parallel to a Forbes family occasion was uncanny. Christmas still looming large throughout Ann's home. I began to understand how much she loved the festivities; the music, the decorations, the tree, the nativity scenes, the crockery – everything. We sat in the beautiful dining room, a room with red carpet, red walls and floor to ceiling bookshelves, stuffed with books, separated by a fireplace.

At the table I took time to absorb the enormity of the occasion. If things had been different, this is the family I would have had countless meals with. These were my sisters and brother, my mother and the man who had once proposed to be my father. I could have grown up in this house, surrounded by vibrant colours and books and history, with a strong sense of self and where I'd come from. The pointlessness of contemplating the string of 'what ifs', scoffed at by many, doesn't stop the rest of us from going there.

The place I grew up suddenly seemed more beige than beige. A new housing estate, 70s red-brick veneer, one bookshelf relegated to one part of the house, the beige carpet and wallpaper – it was comfortable, warm, clean and loving – and beige.

It seemed like dinner as usual for the family. The food was comforting and familiar. The conversation more stilted. I was awestruck. I wanted to stare and analyse their behaviours, how they ate, how they chewed, held their cutlery, what they left on their plate. Everything. I felt somehow aware this occasion may never happen again. I had to soak up every verbal and non-verbal exchange.

Our bed was set up in the dining room. We slept on the red carpeted floor, looking up at the high ceilings, art hanging on the red walls and a glass antique cabinet of my favourite Royal Doulton 'Pansy' china in the corner. As I lay there, holding Andrew's hand, exhausted and exhilarated, I gave utter thanks to everyone who had played a part in bringing me to this point. I mean everyone. I prayed for me and all of my families – past, present and future. I was discovering who I was and where I came from. It was starting to fill the hole that existed deep within my being, the hole I'd covered, that I'd ignored and set aside for another day. That day had come.

We hugged everyone goodbye and thanked them for an unforgettable stay in the family home in Launceston before heading off on a road trip around the beautiful island that took hold of us from that first touch-down, lasting to this day. Our sights set on the west coast we took our time to get there after exploring the solemn beauty of the south. Forests and rivers galore, a special treasure awaited us in Strahan.

My cousin was touted as a like-mind, had spent her undergraduate years studying theatre in Launceston, away from her family home in the Adelaide Hills, was working in hospitality through summer on the west coast until a new year of studies commenced. With a hug to rival the first with Bronwyn a year and a half earlier, my attraction to Emma was instant. She was brilliant of heart and mind and very much a kindred spirit. We connected instantaneously, drinking in as much as we could of each other, and the beverages on tap. We both had our own paths to traverse and conquer and we knew we would intersect many times into our futures. My heart was filling up.

BUILDING CONNECTIONS

Over many years Ann and I developed a type of mother-daughter relationship mixed with a type of woman-to-child relationship and almost a woman-to-woman understanding. There was always a boundary, an invisible line, which at times I overstepped. My own boundaries were clear to me. I wanted Ann in my life so that I could get to know and understand her, so I could be part of the healing she needed after giving me away and my own healing from loss. I wanted her to know me, to see herself in me and to see glimpses of others in me; her mother, her father, her sisters, her children – my sisters, my brother. My father. I never wanted my presence to interfere in her life and at the same time I knew that I interfered in her life decades ago. My presence, my being, disrupted her life and would be a disruption to many more as a result. For good and bad.

I never projected blame or ill will on my biological mother for giving me up, I found gratitude almost everywhere. I was lucky. My mum and dad were lucky because I was 'special'. They chose to have me. She chose to give me away. I was lucky.

I learned what kind of mother Ann was to her subsequent children. She was playful, she worked alongside them, she encouraged a love of literature and art and music. She was a competent piano player and singer. She'd sung in many choirs and was passionate and proficient. We didn't speak about her musical preferences but I know she loved it, as I do.

In our every conversation, whether by phone, email or in person, she amazed me. As the years passed and I understood her more, I began to anticipate her ways. I was sometimes wrong, and she still surprised me, for good and for bad. But overall, I saw some traits emerging.

She was candid, interesting, inspiring and a font of knowledge about so many things. Like me she would collect information, taking notes, cut newspaper clippings, gather pamphlets to keep, or more often she'd pass it on to someone else to whom it would be of interest. So, like me. It was comforting and opened my heart to the knowledge of what I'd been missing. Alikeness. It amplified the unspoken silence, an absence of familiarity. Before I met Ann, I'd been captivated and in a way in love with the fantasy of what could be, who my mother would be, who my father would be. Now that I was getting to know the truth, I realised the comfort and assurance of being around alikeness. The more I had, the more grateful I was to have found her, before it was too late. My wonder evolved.

We have spoken openly about all kinds of things, but rarely matters of the heart and certainly not grief or loss or sadness of any kind. I saw this as her protective layer, given that she'd endured so much loss in her life. I can't imagine what keeping a secret for almost three decades would do to the psyche, could it make a permanent indent on the soul, the spirit? What were the triggers she needed to avoid or respond to in private, without telling anyone why? We never spoke about that, so I filled in the blanks myself. I assumed a lot.

Ann's sharp mind, memory and wit were second to none and her enthusiasm and interest in my life astounded me. In many respects she knew me as an adult woman ten times better than my parents did. To them I remained their child-daughter. To Ann, I was her woman-daughter. She knew my friends, inquired about my work, where I was going, what I enjoyed. She reminded me of things I'd told her, which was reinforced with all that she gave. And she gave.

During my first pregnancy in 1998 a new wave of giving began, which lasted many years. The first wave was a tsunami of parcels that were delivered in readiness for the baby's arrival. Cloth nappies, sheets, blankets, romper suits, singlets from sizes 0000 to 0. They kept coming. My aunt brought over a wicker cane bassinet in which Ann's children had slept – a grand gesture that cracked my heart for her generosity and loss. Although we had nowhere to put the bassinet, I was determined to use it. Of course, the bassinet was a loan and we'd be giving it back after we no longer needed it. I was amazed that she held onto it for so long. It told me more about the person she'd become.

The parcels didn't let up. There were shawls, clothes for all seasons, through all stages from infancy to toddlerhood, to preschool, and through to school. There were toys, books, activities – all posted from her home in Tasmania. Over several years the same parcel post courier delivered the packages to my door. After the first year of deliveries, she asked me, 'What is in these parcels? They're all from the same person.'

I explained they were from my birth mother, with clothing and toys for my baby. We shared a moment to reflect on what that really said about the need for a relinquishing mother to give so much in tangible gifts to her daughter and first grandchildren. I was so grateful. I was overwhelmed. I always called or emailed to thank her for her great taste and generosity. She stated that nothing she bought was at retail price and I admired her even more for her tenacity, research and superb shopping skills.

As I knew Ann loved shopping and bargain hunting, I invited her to join me on a shopping tour to factory outlets, a fundraiser for the local breastfeeding support group. We had a wonderful day with a bunch of women I was getting to know. They were all passionate about their mothering journey, as Ann had been, yet this was the first time we'd shared such a day together. I introduced her to friends as my birth mum, Ann, and I overheard her say to someone in a shop, 'I'm checking this size for my daughter.'

I know we were far from being mother and daughter in the traditional and socialised sense, but that simple recognition, in a few words, was far from simple.

GIVEN A PLACE, BELONGING

Ann and I remained in regular contact. Whenever she was in Melbourne we'd always meet up and spend a good part of the day or evening together, sharing food, stories and experiences. And so it went. For years. It was with great sadness and humility that she included me in the news of the terminal illness of her beloved David. He was a most wonderful man for whom I will always be grateful, a man who easily could've been my father if Ann had decided to accept his proposal back in 1964. He was one person who knew about me and, more importantly, he loved and supported Ann throughout his life.

I was expected to be at his funeral, alongside Ann, Nana, my aunts, uncles and my siblings, Ann and David's children. I was still tentatively navigating my place in the family, especially careful at such a sorrowful and fraught time. The night before the funeral Ann asked me to give the only reading at the funeral, an enormous honour. In many ways I felt like I was the perfect person to do this, in many ways I was an outsider with a unique perspective of the family. It's like I was a hatchling from an egg laid by Ann, raised by Mum and Dad when I learned to fly until I could soar high enough to gain the view from above. I swooped down to meet the family and dropped in on the funeral – but something happened to me while I was there. While the family knew who I was, there were people at David's funeral who didn't know me. My resemblance to Ann and her family is unquestionable – and I'd been invited to stand up in front of all of David's people and give the reading. I introduced myself by name alone and gave the reading. It was an important, public and private acceptance of my place in the family. I felt validated and purposeful and of use. Something shifted for me, but at the time I was too consumed with the wellbeing of Ann and my sister to really take it in.

THE TRUTH OF IDENTITY

I loved being pregnant – I'd waited a long while for it to happen and apart from a mysterious allergy to certain fish and shellfish, the pregnancy was event-free. I loved my changing shape and state of mind, and although there was a lot of uncertainty there were things I knew for sure. The question of my paternity loomed larger on the horizon than ever before. I'd heeded Ann's warning – 'Don't look for him'– for four years. Most of that time I felt quite content with my evolving story and the merging of my past with my present. But things were starting to shift – I needed more, and while I still had Ann's wishes in mind, it was something I needed to follow up. I had a name and little else. When I first met Julie and Gionni and they told me they knew who he was, and it was time they knew that I had a name. I wanted to ask for their help in passing on my details to Silvio.

Andrew took a photo of me pregnant – feeling and looking extra fabulous, dressed up for our friend's wedding. I put it in an envelope with the letter I'd written with great care and consideration. I would post the letter to Julie and Gionni with a request for them to pass it on to the man I knew to be my father.

27th January 1999

Dear Silvio,

It's hard to know where to start with this letter. I've been waiting for this opportunity for so long and I've had the words and stories going around in my head for all that time. Please be assured that I don't want to cause any trouble, I just need the chance to know something about you. It will help me fill in some missing pieces in my own life.

The last few years have been quite incredible, with finding the whereabouts of my birth mother, meeting her and her family including mother, sisters, brother and children. Among all of this I had the fantastic opportunity to meet Julie and Gionni. I can sense what special people they are and I'm very grateful to Julie for her support and understand the memories it has brought closer to her have at times been difficult.

I'm not sure what you know about me and my life, but to quickly bring you up to date – here goes:

My birthday is 8th February and I'll be 34 this year. I grew up in Newcastle in a loving and supporting family. Mum and Dad have been incredible throughout my search, especially Mum, showing me strength, courage and generosity that I didn't know was possible. Ever since I can remember I have been interested in music, movies – most forms of entertainment really, although it's safe to say that

I'm not the 'sporty' type. I left school at fifteen and studied to become a secretary which I did for many years in all kinds of industries including insurance, construction, government, publishing, hospitality and entertainment. I moved to Melbourne when I was twenty to study Drama and gain my HSC equivalent qualification. The last fourteen years in Melbourne have taken me through many stages. I met the wonderful Andrew (Ingram), who I married three years ago. We had lived together for ten years prior to that amazing day. His father is Scottish and mother is Latvian. We bought a house last June and I'm now expecting our first baby in March 1999. Not long to go now, and we're both getting more and more anxious / excited as each day goes by.

In 1993 Andrew and I spent six months travelling to the UK, Europe and US. We had the time of our lives and we hope to do it again one day. I absolutely adored my time in Italy. We caught a train from Paris to Rome, and as I wandered around the train after we'd crossed the France / Italy border other passengers started speaking to me in Italian. Unfortunately, I don't speak the language, but have always had some unexplained affinity with Italian culture.

I've spent considerable time devoted to performing in plays, short films and the like, but decided some time ago to pursue a paid career path in other areas of the entertainment industry. I'm now managing a known band based in Melbourne – they have a record deal and tour regularly, and I'm also a freelance publicist. I set up my own business about four months ago and I work from home which is going really well. I hope to be able to continue, in a part-time capacity at least, after the baby is born. Fingers crossed all goes well.

I couldn't decide which photo to send with this letter, so I put them both in. I'm sure the one from my wedding day will be obvious. The other photo was taken in October when I was four months pregnant.

I'd love to hear from you as soon as you can manage it. I'd especially love a photograph of you, a recent one and one of you in your 20s if at all possible. Obviously I have loads of questions which hopefully you can answer in time. I'm very curious about your background. What region of Italy does your family come from? Do you have any family still living there? What about your family now? Do you have children? What kind of work have you done? Do you still work? When is your birthday? What are your passions in life? Of course I'd love to meet you in the flesh one day, but I shouldn't get too carried away I suppose. I certainly have no intentions of imposing myself onto your family as it is really just you that I need to know about. Anything beyond that would be an absolute bonus. Getting to know you is all that really matters to me. I've believed all my life, until a couple of years ago, that you weren't aware of my existence. Having the chance to write to you is part of my dream coming true.

I hope to hear from you soon. Karen

Up until this point I'd kept in semi-regular contact with Julie and Gionni, mostly through Christmas cards. I knew enough to understand their friendship with Ann and David had waned over the years, without ever knowing why. In a way it helped, as I was more interested in keeping my communication as direct as possible. Ann didn't want me to contact my biological father at all, and by now I really believed I could do it without involving her.

I never heard back from Julie or Gionni.

I was so enamoured with my baby boy Angus that the idea of pursuing Silvio drifted back to the distance, temporarily. Like a boat on the choppy bay, it would rise up now and then, enough for me to notice it was there, it didn't carry me away. Other feelings crept in and caught me unawares. Recurring sleeping and waking dreams for a short time in those early days had a range of scenarios that ended with my beautiful baby being taken from me. I was reflecting on what it must have been like for Ann, to have had given birth and never to have seen her baby, me. When out and about with my baby Angus in a pram, I felt an underlying uneasiness that someone would walk past and lift him out of the bassinet and whisk him away from me. These thoughts and imaginings were rarely expressed.

After a baby is born a collective preoccupation occurs. Family, friends and strangers are compelled to find a familiar physical trait. Being adopted I was acutely attuned. Adopted people are well aware we don't look like anyone in our family, acutely aware when tenuous links are made to our familiarity and likeness to others and we're acutely aware how important it is to... everyone.

'He has your eyes.'
'Who does he look like?'
'He's a real blend of both of you.'
'He's got his dad's chin.'
'He's just like you.'

Before becoming a mother, every one of those remarks shot through me like a dart. I never looked like anyone, so what did people say about me? How come we can't value the attributes of a baby, of a small child, of an adult, that are purely theirs. Why are we so preoccupied with the desire to draw comparisons to likeness? Is nothing our own? Yet when it finally happened to me, I was overjoyed! It brought me great comfort. So when my baby was born and people talked about who he looked like, my smiles were smudged with a melancholy. Ann never spoke to me of her feelings about seeing her grandchild for the first time, or times after that while watching him and our daughter grow into their own skins, as individuals with indelible links to her heritage and the heritage of another man who was unknown to us.

My maternal familial resemblance has been uncanny – not just physical, but some mannerisms and voice patterns as well. The more I got to know the more I wondered. If so much of me is like Ann and her family, what, if anything, do I have that resembles my father? The more I got to know Ann the more I realised how different we were, which made me wonder: which parts of me, who I am, my essence, how I feel and see the world – that is not part of my nurtured experience – can be attributed to my father? So I gesticulate a lot. Is that the Italian bit of me? What about my sense of wonder? My curiosity? My optimism? Where does this come from? Why does it even matter? I can't help but think that if I'm anything like my father, he would definitely want to know me.

My relationships with Ann, my sister and my aunty flourished. We were there for each other and part of each other's lives. When Angus was eleven months old he was hospitalised for five days and kept in isolation. I was with him every day and every night, still trying to manage work phone calls from the corridor in between breastfeeds, cuddles and conversations with doctors. I'll never forget the comfort and love provided by my aunt when she delivered a delicious home cooked meal to the hospital room. It shouted 'family' to me. It was one of many times when I felt connected and that I belonged and that I'd found my people.

My Forbes family was still and always will be my family. They are who I draw my strength and much of my identity from – as problematic as that may be. I haven't lived in the same state as my family for twenty years, and that has come at a cost – for all of us. The disconnection has been significant, and the relationships that I've been allowed to nurture with Andrew's family and my maternal family have been equally significant. These relationships have continued to influence my story, until this day, as do the loving relationships I have with my mum and dad, my brothers, my sisters-in-law (who

I've known most of my life) and their children, my nephews and niece, who I've loved since the days they were born. My identity is complex and incomplete.

Ann has always loved Christmas – she collected many nativity scenes and also sent us a few. The Christmas after David died she was in Melbourne and came along with us to the local Carols in the Park at the end of our street. She openly wept but kept her thoughts silent. I saw her watching my children, her grandson and granddaughter with a deep stare, with love and who knows how much remorse about what could have been. I may well be romanticising, and I may well be placing my own loss and grief onto the woman who gave birth to me – her decision so long ago continues to affect me and, as the pebble is dropped into the pond, the ripples reach me and my children.

Mum had shown so much love and strength during my search for Ann and I was always careful not to flaunt our interactions in front of her. She'd often ask, 'Have you heard from Ann?' I'd always answer honestly and play down all of the gifts and parcels. There's no way Mum could compete, not that she would, but I know it would upset her. Mum would always be in a league of her own. The last thing I wanted to do was to upset her. The last thing I wanted to do was deny my relationship with Ann. The last thing I wanted to do was to hurt or upset anyone. The last thing I wanted to do was pretend the yearning inside me for my truth was nothing.

Mum and Dad came to stay with us soon after we'd moved into our new house. While we didn't realise it at the time, it was to be their last trip to Melbourne, and I look back on that visit with such fond memories, and with a desperate longing for things to be different. I wish we were not separated by distance, by illness and capacity. I wish my kids would know what it's like to visit their Grandma and Grandpa whenever they wanted, and to have them watch them play music and netball, and blow out their birthday candles and to know their friends by name. It was not to be. Mum and Dad's visit coincided with a visit to Melbourne by Ann and, as they'd met several times over the years, and remained firmly on each other's Christmas card lists, I wanted to host an afternoon tea for them all with scones, jam, cream, the good china – the works.

A couple of years after our beautiful, much-loved and wanted daughter Brigit was born, my hair started to curl. While I'd always had an enviable wave, it all changed. Ann also had an enviable head of long hair, one of the many things I loved and admired about her was that as an older woman she was proud to wear her long thick hair out, maybe with a clip, and sometimes up on a warm day, but mostly she let her wild, beautiful hair fly free. This is the complete opposite of my Mum's tidy perm and set 'do' she'd had all of my life and longer. Since my hair started taking on its own free-wheelin' curly style, Mum began to make more regular comments about it. As with my weight, or my choice of clothing, her comments were mostly critical. My hair really bothered her and in the back of my mind I knew why.

The morning of the tea, after I'd baked the scones and set the table, I was ready to drive over to my Bron's to pick up Ann and Madeline. Mum pulled me aside before I left and asked me to tie my hair up, to pull it back, tame it. As a grown woman with two children, I resented being told how to wear my hair by my mother. I thought it was another symptom of me being her child-daughter and I resisted. I'd come a very long way in claiming my emotional and physical being and her asking me to pull back my hair made me dig my heels in.

'I don't want to.'

'Please,' she pleaded.

'But why?' I insisted.

'Because you look too much like Ann.' She said it.
She was confronted by my looks. I was comforted by them. I loved that I looked like Ann. It was too much for Mum.

I left the house with my free-wheelin' hair flying and on my drive to Port Melbourne I dug my heels in further. I would NOT change my hair. I am a grown woman and I love my curls and I love that my hair is like Ann's. Nobody is going to tell me how to wear my hair. For crying out loud!

By the time I pulled up out the front of Bron's house I'd accepted my own compromise. I'd taken a hair tie with me before I flew out of the house. With mixed up feelings of respect and resentment, maybe a touch of rebellion, I tied half of my hair up without impinging on its length. It was my way. Hairstyle or not, I realised that day just how hard it had become for Mum. The morning tea went well, it wasn't awkward, but I started to see how untenable these gatherings were. Who was it for? I had no idea. Ann always seemed eager to meet with Mum and Dad – I'm not sure if she saw them as friends, or custodians of her daughter or what. As it was to be Mum and Dad's last visit to Melbourne, I'm very glad to have not endured a repeat scenario.

Mum and Ann continued to be on each other's Christmas card list for some time, although Mum found Ann's cards a bit much. They were created by Madeline with themes that pushed the envelope in a head-on collision of patriarchy and Christianity. I loved all of Madeline's cards and loved the fact that Ann loved them and continued to send them out, despite her own conservative Christian beliefs. Mum and Dad were reassured when Ann shared their rejection of women priests in the Anglican church. Despite being so different, they had many things in common.

As time slowly ticked by, I thought I was equipped to handle the physical and emotional distances between Mum and Ann's relationships and my own relationships with both of them. On one hand I had a deep connection with the woman who loved, nurtured, and cared for me for my whole life. The woman who I butted heads with and challenged, and whom I felt at times smothered by. On the other hand, I had been gifted a chance of knowing the woman from whom I'd sprung; the woman and familial ties from whom I took unknown elements of my being. This woman moved from beyond a curiosity; I had a deep longing to understand who she was, and for her to understand and know me. She was incredibly interested in me, my life, my work and my friends. We enjoyed many phone calls and I continued to learn her speech patterns, her intonations. I'm sure there were times I didn't actually hear what she was saying because I was so intent on listening to her voice, which called to the depth of my being. This was the voice that I had longed to hear. Not only was she interested in me, she knew so much in a short time about who I was as an adult. We got to know each other as adults, and much of our bonding was fixed in the present. I was careful not to bring up too many aspects of my childhood – I thought it would make her sad to think of what might have been. I kept stories fairly general, 'we went here', or more about my aunts and uncles, my brothers and their wives and their kids. She knew who was important to me, the people I had in my life, and I didn't have to explain anyone to her. The parcels continued to arrive. There were books on all topics; lots of books for the children with worldly themes, practical tips, the literary classics and many narrative, pictorial and musical representations of the Christmas story in particular. For the most part I felt she got me. I felt liberated that she did, and that I didn't need to pretend.

Still there was something missing. As time ticked by, and I managed the relationships around me, I yearned for the unknown. I needed to know who he was. The man whose name she gave me with the warning, 'Do not look for him.' The yearning began to consume me and I knew that I had to do something. And so my search began in earnest.

SEARCH

Methodical searches through phonebooks at the post office came up with nothing. Online searches across all states came up with nothing. My thoughts often visited a sad place – perhaps I'm too late. Perhaps he's dead. That nobody knew of him. That he moved to another country or that my search was over before it began. Something pushed me. I felt compelled to continue on this path. My yearning compelled me. By now my kids were at primary school, I was working three days a week and spent the rest of my time dabbling and volunteering my passion and skills in the community.

The search to find Silvio took me to the electoral office in Braybrook. I expected to find a hive of busy and interesting people beavering away at research projects and data mining. Instead I arrived at an uninspiring building, vacant on the ground floor. A paper sign on the wall directed the way to the electoral office upstairs. Beyond the glass doors at the top of the stairs on level one was a very high counter. I told the person at the desk I was looking for someone. She showed me how to search on one of two computers set up in the foyer. Away I went. Starting in New South Wales, I eventually searched his name in every state. Nothing.

Silvio Nino – where are you? How hard could this be? Every name in the country sat at my fingertips, every name except for the name I wanted. Disheartened I left, thinking something was wrong.

I made the decision to keep Ann out of this picture altogether. I heeded her warning to not look for him for ten years or so, until it became unbearable. With my emphatic belief it was my right to know – or at the very least try and find out – who my biological father was, and encouraged by everyone to this day, I believe it was a natural progression I would make, that most people in my position would take. I was not deterred. I also decided to leave Mum and Dad out of it. They were getting older and after all they'd been through, and all they'd given me by helping find Ann, having Ann in our lives and, in recent times, the challenges they faced in my relationship with Ann, I took up my search without their knowledge. I had loads of love and support and encouragement from Andrew and other treasured friends. More importantly, I had my children, for whom I knew this search would one day be important.

As time ticked by, almost weekly there came reminders and prompts about the importance of family – finding out where you came from. They were everywhere – in films, in the media, in school projects and in conversations with friends. I began hearing and seeing messages in the leaves, in the wind, in the sound of the creek and the birds. My consciousness heightened. I heard it everywhere I went: every time a baby was born, meeting people for the first time, sharing stories of friends who were visiting grandparents and finding out more about their own history. In fact, family history was always popping up in my conversations with Mum. She'd often talk about her time as a child, and what happened to her grandmothers and the lives they lived and the letters they'd left behind, the inheritances that were misplaced, overlooked or taken by someone. Long-lost cousins with blindness and diabetes, it ran in the family.

I was always interested and always imagining her stories were actually connected to me. They weren't, ever. They were all someone else's stories, someone else's connections – not mine. This idea of painting a family tree for my children propelled me. I saw the connections throughout families of every person I knew worn as badges of pride of belonging to a clan, a tribe with a specific family history. This was my search, affecting me and my children. Whenever I got to the point of actually finding him, then it would be about him as well. And as was my intention when I began my search for Ann, I had every intention of keeping it classy, always respectful and discrete. I knew I could do this. And so I did.

It was a huge blow not finding Silvio on the electoral roll. I was stuck. I returned to my folder of papers. The night I'd spent with Ann in Rye with my folder – the night she told me 'Do not look for him' – uncharacteristically, I took no notes. I just sat and listened. Why, oh why didn't I write anything down? Certainly Silvio's name was etched in my mind from that moment onwards.

Most weeks one of us would find the occasion to visit the Italian deli around the corner. Roccos Deli is somewhat of a neighbourhood institution where first-time visitors become regular customers. Rocco and his wife Adriana have been running the deli for decades, selling quality smallgoods with continental flair and verve. Old school. Sometimes a song and often a story, there's always a familial greeting from both of them. They know us well and so many of the local families and customers. Photos of the children and grandchildren in the neighbourhood adorn the walls behind the register. Everyone loves going to Roccos. Not long after my electoral-roll fiasco I was in there on a mid-week day, the only customer in the store with some time to spare. So a conversation began. Rocco and Adriana quizzed me on where I was from, apart from being from Newcastle. They sensed something was up. I told them I was adopted and that I'd met by birth mother. Responding to their questions, I revealed more. I told them my father was Italian and I didn't know who he was. The story of my search thus far emerged. The two of them stood side by side, hanging on my words with such intent. Looking into their eyes it felt as if my story was as important to them as it was to me. After hearing of my roadblock, the suggestions came thick and fast.

Rocco insisted I had the wrong name.

'Are you sure? Did you write it down when she told you?' I convinced them I was sure of the name. Nah, nah, nah Rocco wasn't having it.

'Karen, Nino isn't a surname, it's a first name. You try Nino D'Silva!'

They told me I must go back to the electoral role and look up this new name. Something was definitely wrong with the name Silvio Nino.

And so I did. I went back to the electoral role, now feeling more like a pro, more like a PI fact-checking for a client – except the client was me. I typed 'D'Silvia N' in the search field and there were several listings that came close, but not quite. I was still using the information I'd secured from that conversation with Ann (that he had a son called Anthony) and from Julie and Gionni years earlier (they knew who he was and he lived not far from their house in Lane Cove in Sydney). These two pieces of information were vital in my search. This electoral-roll thing was not cutting it for me. What was wrong?

I returned to my original memory of hearing his name from Ann. Silvio Nino. Maybe I was spelling it all wrong. I tentatively typed the letters, Nin and, New South Wales... the screen reloaded and a raft of names beginning with Nin appeared before me. I scrolled down and found... Silvio Ninni, Maxine Ninni and Benjamin Ninni listed at the same address, and below, Anthony Ninni. My heart was racing. Upstairs in a nondescript, uninspiring building in Braybrook, at the urging of my Italian friends Rocco and Adriana from their deli around the corner, I pieced together the information, and finally, bingo! I found his name. Checking the proximity of the listed address to that of Julie and Gionni's, I was without a doubt that I had found him. Awash with adrenaline and self-congratulations I couldn't get home fast enough to get cracking in front of my own computer.

By the time Andrew arrived home from work I had a photo of Ben Ninni and the supposition that he was my brother, still living at home; and that Anthony, his older brother, my other brother, would be a few years younger than me and probably living at his own address, with his own family. I tried to keep a lid on my excitement. Andrew and I sat down to talk and dissect the information I'd gathered – wondering aloud late into the night. I decided I'd let this latest turn of events settle for a night or two and then consider what I'd put in a letter to Silvio.

18 November 2011

Dear Silvio,

I am writing to you as I believe you to be my biological father and it is with respect that I contact you after so many years. This is a difficult letter to write and I can imagine not an easy letter for you to read.

For so long I have put the concerns and feelings for others ahead of my own needs, however the time has come for me to follow through on what I can no longer ignore. The fact that I have blood relatives whom I've never made contact with, let alone met, leaves a gaping hole in my life, my family, my history and my future.

My intuition is getting louder and clearer every day – that I must reach out to you, and give you the opportunity to know me, your daughter. Beyond that, now that I am a mother, it means that you have a twelve year-old grandson, Angus, and a nine year-old granddaughter, Brigit. They are both very proud to have Italian blood running through their veins, and while they learn Italian at school and are extremely fond of Italian food (who wouldn't be?) they have had little exposure to genuine Italian culture and experiences.

Family is important to us all and many heartfelt conversations with my children have influenced me in contacting you. We all go through times when we want to gain deeper understanding of who we are and where we come from. A sense of identity, background and heritage is important. This is why I need to connect with you, for myself, for my children and for you and your family. I write to you without anger, but with hope.

I'm married to a wonderful supportive man, Andrew. We have been together for 26 years, and married for 16. In 1993 we travelled to Europe, UK and US. We hope one day to return to England and Italy and go to Spain for the first time.

When I was younger I studied drama and performed with community theatre companies. I worked for many years in the music and arts industry managing bands, tour promotion, as a publicist and teacher of artist management. The music business wasn't conducive to the lifestyle of parenting, so gradually my focus shifted – although I'm occasionally drawn back to event management and publicity.

I've spent the past ten years as a volunteer for the Australian Breastfeeding Association as a community educator and counsellor and have been a media spokesperson for them for four years. I've done lots of interviews in press, radio and television. Maybe you've seen me on the TV without knowing who I was!

While continuing to volunteer I'm also a registered civil celebrant and have officiated at a range of ceremonies – weddings, namings, house-warmings and funerals. You can see some photos of me at work on my website.

I work part-time at a community health service that harnesses my passion for the rights of migrants, refugees and Indigenous Australians. This year I started studying at university, part-time, BA – Community Development.

Above all of this, I love music, I love a good laugh, I love to eat great food and spend time with people I care about. I'm easy going and I'm an optimist.

As you'll see my life is very full and I am so fortunate to have the support, love and encouragement of my husband and children, which enables me to follow my passions. Even with my full life, there is still a space I have for you.

I dearly hope for a response from you Silvio. I dearly hope that you can acknowledge that I am a result of your actions, from a long time ago (I was born on 8 February 1965). I dearly hope that you can find a way to reconcile the needs of you and your family with the needs of me and mine.

I realise that you may not have made any mention of me to your family and understand how this will be difficult for you and of course you will need some time to process this information. If you would like to discuss this with your family before you reply to me, I completely understand. However, you are welcome to contact me in the meantime and I assure you of my discretion.

Otherwise, if you are not interested in making contact with me at all, and I don't hear from you by Easter 2012, I would like to begin to make discreet contact with my brothers, Anthony and Ben. They too are my family and we all have much to gain by knowing each other.

Andrew, Angus, Brigit and I will be spending Christmas in Newcastle with my family, and some time afterwards in and around Sydney. If there is any chance we could meet, please let me know.

I look forward to hearing from you. Karen

I stared at these words for a day, let them sit, checked and rechecked. With a couple of changes made and carefully selected photos printed, on Sunday afternoon I walked two blocks to the closest post box. I felt enormous relief, power and responsibility around this moment of arrival, which had been more than ten years in the making. Once the letter was dropped into the box, I knew there was no turning back. Hearing the envelope drop onto the others inside the box synchronised with my beating heart and again as I let the handle go. Stopping for a brief moment, my steps towards home were heavy with the enormity of what might happen next, yet my heart soared among the treetops. My head, meanwhile, was busy anticipating what would be next and how long I'd be waiting for a response. I knew in my heart of hearts that once I found him I had to make contact. I didn't want to retract the letter or stop the mail. I wanted Silvio to receive the letter. With all my heart I hoped he would receive it in the spirit with which it was intended.

Wednesday night was warm and we'd just finished dinner when my phone rang. While I wasn't expecting anyone to call, I had a strange feeling. I froze and couldn't answer it. I didn't recognise the number and thought I should listen to the message and allow me time to process what was said. It was Ben. I couldn't tell if he was angry or not – he played it very cool. The message went along the lines of:

'Hello Karen, it's Ben Ninni here. You sent a letter to my dad which he received today. Can you please call me on—?'
I played it a couple of times and Andrew heard it as well. We both agreed it was impossible to tell the sentiment behind the message. Was it:

'What the hell have you done?'

'Who the fuck do you think you are writing to my dad like that?'

'Oh my god – you are my sister!"

'You've got the wrong address.'
It could have been any one of those as far as we knew. I had to call back. I felt sick to the core, my hands began to sweat, but I knew. I needed to do it, I'd worked hard for it, it was my right and my heart's desire. It was showtime. I dialled.

REVELATION

Incredibly it was the most wonderful outcome I could have hoped. It turns out Ben was no Hells Angel who wanted to blow my brains out! He told me first up that the letter nearly gave his dad a heart attack. That was my worst fear — what shock such a letter would give the man who never suspected or expected me. I was really concerned. Ben explained the effect the letter had on his dad and his mum as well as his brother Tony. He explained the deep shame Silvio felt from this revelation. He did not deny having an affair with Ann. Ben asked me to tell him what I knew of what had happened all that time ago, which I did. He was starting to sound excited that indeed my story checked out with what his father had told him. His brother Tony however was very concerned and suspicious of my contact. I understood completely — in fact I had to anticipate that response from the whole family. While my story seemed to check out Ben asked, with some hesitation, if I would consider having a DNA test, which I agreed to without any hesitation, as I'd also anticipated this. I asked him about his mum. After Silvio I was most concerned for the woman who would be receiving this letter as proof of her husband's infidelity, although they weren't married at the time. I recalled

Ann's words: 'It's complicated, he had a girlfriend, they went on to marry and have a child, a son called Anthony.'

Ben's explanation was music to my ears. I was delighted to hear, while getting an awful shock, that his mother was a beautifully wise woman who completely understood my need to know who my father was, as she'd undertaken a similar search of her own later in life. I told Ben how grateful I was to hear that and happy to know that Silvio would have the support and understanding of his wife, as I would've hated him to deal with this on his own. Ben asked me about my kids and was excited to hear about them. He told me about his fiancé and their wedding plans. Then he paused and said, 'Wow, so you could be my sister!' and my breath disappeared.

It was true. Yes, indeed I could. We made loose plans to stay in touch, and I suggested we meet up for a coffee when we were in Sydney in the new year, in a month or so. 'Oh we can definitely have a coffee,' he said.

Christmas was coming and I was so excited to be spending it in Newcastle with my family. We were going by car, up the Hume and back to make the most of our time. We would save money on car hire and spend the savings on accommodation nestled within my familial heartland, Bar Beach. Back to the place where my childhood dreams took to my subconscious heights, soaring above the rooftops, up and around the jagged coastline, towards industrial land, town and beach. My only plan for that holiday was to enjoy every moment by being in the moment, not portending the future or wishing anything other than what was. I wanted to spend each moment with Mum and Dad, authentically theirs, strengthening our connection. My intent never needed be articulated to anyone. It was a wonderful Christmas sprinkled with hilarious times with the kids, beach time, cliff time and fireworks viewed from the Obelisk on the hill, a maritime marker. Mum and Dad came over for lunch and we hung out at our place, as I imagined we would often do had only I lived within their reach. Instead we all make do with carefully plotted and crafted updates, trying to pick up where we left off. It's imperfect and flawed and over the years of living so far apart, it usually leaves me feeling guilty or sad. Often both. When holiday time 'at home' works well, it's the best; it embellishes the romantic place I've reserved for my hometown, a place that will never be rivalled by person, place or other people's memories. Places all over Newcastle are etched into my spirit, which I'm able to visit no matter where I am, and when I'm physically there, I drop in so as to brighten the colour and depth of the etchings I carry within me.

MEETING

Before we left Newcastle bound for Sydney I sent Ben a text.

31/12/2011 3.30pm
Hi Ben, we'll be in Sydney from afternoon of Monday 2/1 and leaving Thursday morning 5/1. If you have any time to meet up for a coffee or drink in that time let me know. I hope your family had a lovely Christmas and that you have fab party plans for tonight. ☺ Karen.

I left two voicemail messages over three days and became rather worried he had changed his mind and he didn't want to know me after all. While I managed to switch off from the impending excitement during our holiday in Newcastle, that last day the valve was loosened, bleeding excitement and anxiety all over me. We settled in at my brother's that first night and planned a day of sightseeing the next day, yes, for the kids but also I needed a major distraction from what was (not) happening. We walked around Circular Quay, had some lunch and I contemplated whether I should leave another message for Ben. Tomorrow was our last day in Sydney and I felt no control over the time racing ahead without me. As we waited to hop onto the monorail, I decided quickly to leave another message.

3/1/2012 2.44pm
Hi Ben, just wondering if you received my last txt from a few
days ago. We have one more day in Sydney – maybe we
could catch up. Cheers, Karen

The mobile reception wasn't great and I hoped for the best that it got through. I felt sick and wanted to tread really lightly so as not to rock the boat and cause distress or even a disaster. I was so careful and at the same time loved the excitement of being on the monorail with my kids, weaving above the streets of the city I'd idolised my whole life – the unreachable and unattainable Sydney. I romanticised every visit and every idea of ever living there, which was a great distraction. We got off at Darling Harbour with promises of ice creams and boats. My phone rang – it was Ben. As soon as I saw his name my stomach went ping, my heart went pong. I didn't want to sound too excited because he may have news I didn't want to hear. Yes, he still wanted to meet me for a coffee and yes, he could do it tomorrow. I was so excited and could hear in his voice that he was too, which made me feel a million bucks.

'Where will we meet?' I asked.

'Where are you staying?'

'In Parramatta, but we have a car so I could meet you anywhere really.'

'Well, given that you are half-Italian, I think we should meet in an Italian part of town.'

Those innocent words rose up from my heart to my head; they meant the world to me. He was acknowledging a part of my history that had barely been uttered by anyone else, not only that, he was welcoming me into that part of myself, and a part in which we shared.

'Fantastic!' I said. 'Text me the name and the address of the place.'

'How's 11?'

'Perfect!' – I could barely believe my ears.

'So will I get to meet your kids?' he asked.

I was so thrilled that meeting my kids was important to him, but didn't expect them to meet so soon. At the same time, it was a bit like, if not now, when? We were leaving for Melbourne the day after tomorrow.

'I would love you to meet our kids, yes!' And then I added, 'How about you and I meet for a coffee first and then Andrew and the kids can come a bit later. Is that ok?'

'Yes, yes,' he replied and followed with, 'It will just be me; my dad isn't up to meeting you yet, he's still very much in shock and feels a lot of shame.'

'Absolutely, that's perfectly fine.' And I absolutely meant it. 'Ben, I'm just really happy that I get to meet you – I can't wait!'

While we'd been talking on the phone I'd moved around and away from Andrew and the kids to hear what he was saying, and to concentrate. I was smiling, I was walking in circles and ended up next to a pylon beneath the enormous span of Pyrmont Bridge. When I hung up I looked up and didn't know where I was, but it didn't matter. I was flying! So very happy and excited, all fear and dread slipped away. He was so beautiful. I already loved him.

We were back at my brother's place contemplating what was to come tomorrow. I was painting my nails when I received a text.

Café Gioia: 126A Norton Street, Leichardt 11am. I have a surprise for you. See you then ☺

I nearly died. My mind exploded with the thought of a surprise. I wrote:

Sounds perfecto! If not a little nerve racking. I'm up for it tho. ☺

Ben replied:

Haha we'll all be fine I promise lol

Waking up to a hot, sticky Sydney morning would normally provide every reason to bunker down and not leave the house. I find sweltering summers loathsome. But on this morning, adrenaline fuelled me, which didn't make for a relaxed, easy-going pace getting ready in a house full of people. My brother and nephew were off for a big day to watch the cricket and were packing their sandwiches and drinks. I was just trying to have a shower and get dressed, something I do every day of the year, but for some reason every decision to do with my hair, my jewellery, or my shoes was monumental. As was my wont and need, I oversaw what the kids were wearing. Casual and not try-hard. Comfortable yet gorgeous. I knew it was hot outside, but figured the car was air-conditioned and it was really just getting from the car to the cafe. I opted out of make-up as there might be a tear or two, but I didn't compromise on my red lippy.

Off we went. I was navigating by Google maps and trying hard to communicate with Andrew, who has the patience of a saint. My brain was frenetic and scattered. I was afraid and excited. Andrew and the kids would have a muck-around in the playground down the road from the cafe and I'd call him in an hour to meet us. He dropped me off on the nearest corner. I needed to focus on Ben and not think about the surprise at all. Walking through the open terrace of the cafe I looked to see if anyone was sitting outdoors. Thankfully there wasn't, because the heat was already stifling at 11am. I entered through the doorway and was greeted by a beautiful man with a beaming smile and outstretched arms.

'Karen!'

Ben and I hugged, I'm sure he sensed how nervous I was. He seemed so relaxed. Actually, he also seemed pretty excited. He gestured to a table and as my eyes followed I saw a beautifully dressed gentleman standing next to a very attractive lady. They were looking at me. She was smiling. Ben introduced me:

'Karen, this is Silvio.'

Finally, I'd come face-to-face with the man whose name I'd known for ten years, and whose existence I'd known about but not dared to think about since I was eight years old. The man with the name I'd heard, and searched for and couldn't find. The man I found, who received my words in a letter not that long ago, and learned about me for the first time. Here he was. Here I am. Here we are. We hugged and gave each other a kiss on each cheek. His eyes were twinkling with what could've been tears. The attractive woman came to me. Silvio introduced me to his wife Maxine. She was a dream come true! Her smile, and warmth, her open arms, and as I found out later, her open heart – she could make me start believing in angels!

Silvio had the kindest face I'd ever seen. In one way I was in familiar territory, the meeting of family who were looking at me as I was looking at them, with wonder and curiosity, sadness and joy. Coffees were ordered and we began talking. I was surprised by Silvio's very thick Italian accent, and whether it was due to emotion and nerves I wasn't sure, but he reverted to Italian more than speaking in English. At times Ben and Maxine interpreted my words or translated his Italian to English for me. He couldn't believe how much I looked like Ann. He admitted his shame and wanted me to assure him I'd had a good life. He wanted to know why Ann didn't ever tell him she was pregnant. He wondered aloud how she could give her baby away to strangers. He asked over and over, 'Why didn't she tell me?'

I couldn't answer his questions about her, but our animated conversation was barely stilted or awkward. We all had so many questions and so much to say. Maxine was wonderful and put me at ease immediately. I had no idea that she would have so much information to contribute to my story. Maxine and

Ann had been friends. They were both girls from the country, Maxine from Tamworth and Ann from Newcastle – both had moved to Sydney to attend university. It was 1962, Maxine was on a teaching scholarship and Ann was studying pharmacology. As were all of the country girls, they were accommodated in a somewhat supervised or chaperoned boarding house. Maxine described Ann as attractive and gregarious, very intelligent and a lot of fun. She said they were good friends.

News of their friendship started to make a lot of sense to me. No wonder it was, as Ann described it, 'complicated.' She slept with her friend's boyfriend and became pregnant. No wonder she was able to follow their story and find out they went on to marry and have a son. It made so much sense.

Maxine described many times when they went out together having fun and dancing to the bands at supper clubs. It was Ann who encouraged Maxine to go out with her and Julie, and it was Ann who introduced Maxine to Silvio and his best friend Frank and their wider circle of friends. All of the Italian musicians were as entranced by the Australian girls as the girls were enamoured by the suave and well-dressed Italians. Maxine asked me if I'd like to see what Silvio looked like back then, and pulled out a photo from her handbag. It was a calling card that Maxine and Silvio used when they were travelling and meeting new people. It was a business card with their contact details on the back and, on the front, the most divine black-and-white photo of a young Silvio and Maxine. It appeared Silvio had always been a sharp dresser, even this image of them both sitting on the grass showed his suaveness and relaxed, youthful demeanour. What was even more amazing about this pivotal photograph was that it had been taken in Ann's parent's backyard, in Bar Beach. I couldn't believe it. Maxine told me she'd met Ann's family and remembered her parents quite well. Ann had taken them back home a few times on weekend adventures, taking the Italians to Newcastle for some sightseeing.

Another element of the story I had never considered was that Silvio had also walked the footpath and driveway of the Wrightson Avenue house – I never imagined in my wildest dreams that this would be the case.

Maxine and I hit it off and while she was telling stories I glanced across the table to see a quiet Silvio, still with tears twinkling in his eyes. He was reflecting. I checked in with him to see he was ok. He had met me, the daughter he didn't know he had. He couldn't believe it, yet he believed it. He had so many questions for Ann. I told him that she didn't know I was making contact and that she'd warned me against it. He asked me how I found him. I'd mentioned Julie and Gionni, about a letter I sent them a long time ago and asked if he received it. He said he didn't. I told him about the electoral roll, that I had the wrong name and my long talk with Rocco and Adriana.

Maxine interrupted to tell me how she knew we'd get along. The photo I'd sent Silvio had me wearing amber beads given to me by Andrew's mum. Maxine adores amber and spotted my beads immediately. She was incredibly excited and had told her closest friends about me and shown them my photo. She loved my letter and explained the shock and hurt she felt upon reading it, finding out for the first time of her husband's infidelity before they were married. Then she explained how difficult their courtship was. Her parents were furious that she had fallen for an Italian Catholic. They were strict Protestants, Methodists from rural New South Wales and they were not having a bar of it. They were going to make sure that Maxine and Silvio separated, for good. Sadly for the couple, the stress put on them, particularly Maxine, by her family, did mean that their courtship was interrupted several times. Maxine was being called back home to Tamworth, ending the relationship, but later she returned to Sydney where their love would be rekindled. They both sacrificed a great deal to be together and the times were confusing. This made more sense of what I knew of my beginning, as told to me in scant detail by Ann.

Silvio started to explain that it was on one of these breaks from Maxine, when he was feeling low and despondent about their future as a couple, that he and Ann spent time together. He had always regarded her as a good friend and they shared many friends and fun times. Ann was also feeling down as she'd realised the guy she liked, whom I believe to be Silvio's friend Frank, was not interested. Ann told me that night in Rye that she ended up with the wrong man, not the one she really wanted. Again, Silvio's version of events seemed to match perfectly with what I'd known, and the gaps I didn't know were being filled with a rich, complex and timeless story of youthful attraction, love, lust and loneliness. It was a time of the sexual revolution, when women began to demand the freedom to be educated and to question and challenge their roles beyond daughter and wife. A time when cultures clashed and the religious divide was growing between Catholics and Protestants in a changing Australian society. It was a time when the threat of war and conscription politicised young men and women. This was the time into which I was born.

The four of us talked for a long time, time enough to have a coffee, some water and the order of another coffee fulfilled. Suddenly Silvio asked, 'So where are the children?'

Of course! I had forgotten about Andrew and the kids, in the park, with no shade, on a boiling hot January day in Sydney. I called him straight away. They were still alive, albeit sweltering, but they had left the playground and were enjoying an ice cream down the road from the cafe. Eagerly I told them they were wanted at the cafe pronto to meet Ben, Silvio and Maxine. And with those words Andrew knew exactly the enormity of the situation. He had been in my heart every step of the way, and the meeting would be huge for him as well as for our children.

The phone call gave all of us a reason to have a break, go to the toilet and regroup. It was obvious the four of us were very excited. Silvio gestured with two arms and asked, 'Lunch?'

So it was decided we'd settle in for pizza. Just after the waiter took our order, Andrew and our children arrived. Silvio and Maxine didn't have grandchildren, and the looks on their faces when they greeted my son and daughter, as grandparents met grandchildren, filled my heart. There were more tears and fewer words as we looked at each other in wonder. We huddled around the table, wriggling into our seats with excitement and anticipation. Ben and Andrew and Angus all talked about their shared passion for music. They were talking, laughing and showing each other photos on their phones. Brigit hung close to me and was really happy when the pizza arrived. We had red wine and pizza while we sweltered. The cafe was not air-conditioned, as I'd anticipated, and I felt my face sliding onto the floor into a sweaty puddle. It had been an intense, emotional morning charged with a mix of adrenaline, caffeine and wine – a heady combination for such a hot day. Maxine asked about our plans for the rest of the day and, as we'd packed our bathers and towels in the boot of the car, we had it in mind to head to Bondi Beach for a swim. Not because Bondi is awesome, but because Angus and Brigit knew from the reality TV show *Bondi Rescue*.

'Oh no,' grimaced Maxine, 'You don't want to go to Bondi, do you?'

She told us about Shark Beach at Nielson Park, a beautiful place to go for a swim, a place they used to take their boys where they enjoyed many social gatherings and special times with loved ones. I was most grateful for her suggestion, which possibly had layered extra meaning on top, imagining me and my children swimming in the same waters as my father and his other children over past decades. With my wiring overheating I was super keen for a swim. We agreed it would be a great idea and everyone was delighted.

We briefly recapped some of the earlier conversation for Andrew's benefit but for now our beautiful meeting, from coffee to lunch with wine, was coming to an end. We all had a lot to process. Maxine checked in with Silvio in Italian and said to me semi-quietly, not to the whole table, 'Well, my dear, it really does seem like we're family.'

I agreed whole heartedly, yet knew that I'd given Ben an assurance when we first spoke that I'd arrange to have a DNA test. I brought it up so that Maxine didn't have to. While we both thought it was silly in a way because our stories were indisputably linked, we thought it would be best anyway. I offered to make arrangements. Maxine and Silvio both told me it was just a formality. Everyone agreed, and we left on most wonderful terms. Maxine pressed the photo – their young selves on the back lawn of my grandparent's house in Bar Beach – into my hand. We all knew we'd have more to share to continue our connection forever more. We all knew how momentous this occasion had been. The waiter was asked to take our photo, which I promised to send Maxine and Silvio as soon as I could. And I did, and I framed that beautiful, monumental family photo, the first of many. On that day at Café Gioia we all fell head over heels in love.

We drove through bumper-to-bumper traffic as it snaked around Bondi, and I navigated our way away from the hideous surrounds of Bondi Beach in 32 degrees. As the traffic thinned out somewhat, we found ourselves on curved suburban roads. We could sense something wonderful was about to happen, like a magical moment in a place where none of us had been. Maxine was right, there was plenty of shade at Nielson Park thanks to the planting of divine fig trees over a century ago, the change rooms were other-worldly, the crowds had thinned out and we walked to the shore of Shark Beach. Before us was the most idyllic harbour beach, offering beautiful clear water and gentle waves courtesy of passing ferries and sailing boats. It was the coolest, most refreshing and spiritually cleansing swim I've had in my life. I continued my imaginings that we were all being cleansed and soothed and swayed by the same waters that cleansed and soothed and swayed my father's family decades before. It was with relief and surrender that I dipped my entire body beneath the water. I gave in to the tide and floated in water that supported me and that would carry me to my destiny. I had just had the most mind-bending, heart-mending day, a day which I'd imagined, but never the way it turned out. I had only anticipated meeting Ben for coffee, but got so much more. My children had met my father, their grandfather, and we'd been welcomed into their lives. The water lowered my temperature and my heart rate, and I began to feel my centre. I was refreshed and alive and the world felt full of colour and completeness. Another arrival.

Back home at my brother's place we all gathered with tales from the incredible to the mundane about our day. All stories were gratefully given, heard and received and, while I told part of what I was experiencing, I was mindful of how it might be taken by my family. I was asking everyone to keep this between us. It was really important that Mum and Dad didn't find out about what I was going through; I didn't want them to worry and, most importantly, I didn't want to hurt them. That night we finished off an unforgettable holiday at a superb Japanese restaurant close to home – so we could build up our appetite on the walk there and savour the taste on the walk back.

The next day, in the car with Andrew and our children – our beautiful family, closer than ever – we headed south from Sydney, down the Hume Highway. The world seemed different to me. I was heading home to a place full of my things, with friends and people I love waiting to hear the news from my meeting with Ben. I couldn't believe how vivid the colour of the grey bitumen appeared, or the white markings on the road. It hadn't been that long since we drove in the other direction. Everything I could see was vibrant in colour – the car's interior, my dress and my toes. When we arrived home the colours of everything in our home had a new intensity and I had an overwhelming sense of contentment. I felt in full contact with myself. We had dinner with friends and I regaled them with the story. I met up with some more friends and as they asked, I told them too. Andrew and I mulled things over, the kids asked more questions and I did what I could to record and capture these moments. I hadn't thought too much about Ann beyond keeping my new discovery separate from my relationship with her. I popped in to see Rocco and Adriana and gave them an update, in between customers coming and going, and when I returned to work the following week, what had been a turbulent environment was suddenly calm. Or maybe it was me. It was great for me to tell and retell the story, it affirmed what had happened as my truth, and something that happened to me and to others. So much of the imagining had ceased to be. Similar to when I found Ann, there was a loss in the imaginings as more of her story was revealed. Being lost in your imagination can be a creative yet lonely place. I didn't feel alone anymore, I'd collected more people who were part of my story, to continue the ride with me. Naively I thought that once people saw what it had done for me, they would understand and either step back and allow me the freedom of this discovery, or stand by my side.

10 January 2012

Dear Silvio and Maxine,

It was really lovely to meet with you and Ben last week. Thank you so much. I had a lot to process over the past week, as I'm sure you have, and Andrew and I have had a lot to talk about. Angus and Brigit were also excited to meet you. Angus commented several times later in the evening, 'I've had the best day.'

I'm sorry I didn't get to meet Tony and I hope we'll have the chance to meet in the future.

We ended up following Maxine's excellent tip to go to Nielson Park – you were right, Bondi Beach was overwhelming and we had no chance of finding a car park. Our swim at the harbour beach was just beautiful and provided a fitting end to a significant day.

To follow up with your request for a DNA test, I've sourced a company based in Melbourne, which has been recommended to me by a friend who uses them in his legal practice. There is more information about them on the following pages.

As I have placed the order the two kits will be sent to me, one for 'father,' one for 'child.' I will forward Silvio his kit which will have all of the instructions. I understand it will be three x saliva swabs. We return our own samples in the pre-paid envelope provided and await individual notification of the results.

That is as much as I can tell you for now. It will be an uneasy wait for me until these results come through, however I've waited a long time to arrive at this point and I hope the end is in sight.

Thank you once again for the kindness you have shown me and my family.

Best wishes,

Karen

CHAIN REACTION

January was busy – kids back to school, my favourite birthday season was upon us and I had to arrange the DNA test. I began treading the waters in a whole new area, stuff surely reserved for soap operas and detective shows, or the family court. Although it was something that I'd always imagined doing one day, I had absolutely no idea how to go about organising a DNA test. Thankfully a friend with more knowledge in the world of paternity testing referred me to a laboratory in Fitzroy, and Silvio and I were set to take the 'Peace of Mind' test. Our kits arrived in the post to our homes. Me in Melbourne, he in Sydney. The plan was for us to individually return the tubes containing giant cotton buds of our swabbed saliva to the laboratory in Fitzroy. I was not perturbed by any of it, just another great soapie moment; (American accent) 'I'm doing a DNA test to find out the truth, to find out once and for all, who is my biological father.'

I sat on my bed, fascinated by the process and the instructions as my mind wandered to the millions of scenarios that led people to take such tests. Following each instruction with the greatest of care I thoroughly swabbed the saliva from my mouth onto the giant cotton bud and carefully placed it inside the tube, inside another tube, inside a carefully labelled envelope along with the paperwork, and then another envelope. All the while feeling a strong connection with Silvio in Sydney, who I knew was doing the same thing, assisted by Maxine.

I'd read the instructions over and over and noticed they said something about keeping the sample away from extreme temperatures, so became concerned about posting the samples during the stifling heat of summer. I couldn't bring myself to drop this precious envelope into the baking red metal mailbox, to wait hours for collection from a postal worker – oblivious as to the precious nature of the cargo they were moving – driving a red metal van. My best option was to drive my sample to the lab in Fitzroy in the air-conditioned comfort of my car. My imagination anticipated an arrival through the security doors met with congratulatory fanfare or at least a heartfelt acknowledgement of what had brought me to this point. There were definitely security doors, but my precious DNA sample was unceremoniously handed to an anonymous and moderately enthusiastic technician. Again, my mind wandered to the stories that lie within that lab, the stories withheld, unknown, revealed or concealed. Job done. Results would take 2–3 weeks so I just did it and forgot about it – spending the rest of January in various states of holiday mode, back to work mode, holiday and my birthday celebration mode, as well as getting our boy ready for high school.

Brigit had already begun her year at primary school and I had one last day with Angus before his epic adventure at a new school. We decided to have a go trying out the bus route from home to school including the interchange in Footscray. It was a small step beyond our comfort zone and I knew it wouldn't take long before he'd be doing it with a bunch of friends without even thinking. Rushing around the house getting ready to leave I heard the loud clunk of our letterbox lid drop as the postie delivered mail. Another warmer than warm day, I ran out to the box and brought the mail inside. Unsurprisingly I had another flash of 'soap-opera moment' at the sight of the envelope from the DNA lab, which I presumed was the test results. Angus was finishing getting ready and I sat at the kitchen table, thumbing through the other pieces of mail. I returned to the envelope from the lab, carefully opening it, I unfolded the letter inside and read:

```
The DNA Parentage Testing Procedure report
showing that Silvio Ninni is NOT the
biological father of Karen Ann Ingram.
```

BREATHLESS

The planet jerked to a halt.

Frozen.

Re-read it.

Couldn't breathe.

Couldn't believe.

I must. This is science. Science doesn't lie. There's been a mistake.

Staring through the letter to the floor, my mind went straight to Silvio.

What have I done?

I had dropped a live bomb, exploding into the lives of a beautiful family, people who, moments before I opened this envelope, I believed to be my family.

I've created a giant mess.

I'm so sorry.

How can this be?

I called Andrew, speaking in a tight, breathless and pained whisper, 'It's not him, it's not Silvio.'

'What? What do you mean?'

'I got the results back. He's not my father.'

Silence.

Staring into space, my breathing gradually returned, although very shallow. Angus called out, 'Mum, are you ready?'

'Yep.'

We had to keep it moving. I picked up my bag, keys, phone and put on my sunnies. Together we left the house and headed for the bus stop. I said nothing. He walked ahead of me and casually called over his shoulder,

'Hey did you do that DNA test with Silvio?'

What did he know, did he sense something? I couldn't look at him as I replied, 'Yes I did – just got the results.'

'Oh really?'

Softly, I struggled with the words, 'Yep. There was no match. It's not Silvio.'

My beautiful wise boy knew how I'd be feeling. He didn't ask questions, he just put his arm around my shoulders and we walked together, my head hanging low.

I had to get my shit together, after all I was the grown up. We needed to make sense of these buses and this was our last chance for me to understand what was going on, in a world where I could barely understand anything anymore. I rose up and carried on and savoured every moment with my boy and together we hopped on the first bus. By the time we got to Footscray I was managing to lift my downward gaze to look up and around, and pay attention to what was happening. The abstract of time was out of sync, I was operating on an altered plane, I didn't have many words to spare and felt a long way from anyone, except for my darlings, Andrew, Angus and Brigit. We were solid. That's all I knew for sure. The bus was stopped in

Barkly Street and I was getting lost staring at the people waiting on a bench seat outside the market. A crinkled and bony elderly Vietnamese man with a conical hat; a squatty short-statured Greek widow, her head in a black triangular scarf tied tightly under her chin; an African woman with three young children; a well-worn man and woman each sitting on their VB esky. All from different worlds, waiting for the same bus. I managed a smile. Turning my head, I looked out the window on the other side of the bus to see a most beautiful African teenager, her head full of miniature braids falling to her waist, she was rollerblading up the centre of Barkly Street, without a helmet or care in the world. For a moment I was transported to the worlds of these people with whom I probably had more common with than anyone else. Shared moment. Shared place. My heart had been ripped out and I was suspended in space, with very long strings attached to Andrew and the kids, far, far away.

The kids. What have I done to them? I never ever would have put them in the situation of meeting and falling in love with Silvio, Maxine and Ben if I thought there was ANY risk of Silvio not being my biological father. I was devastated for them. I would never risk my kids' emotional security like that. What have I done?

With Angus by my side, when I was meant to be by his, I muddled my way through the bus routes and finally home. I was relieved, but I couldn't speak. I barely spoke for days. And I couldn't shit. I was frozen stiff inside and out. Paralysed. Atrophied.

I wanted to connect with Silvio and Maxine, but a phone

call was out of the question. I may have found the words difficult but my voice was gone. So I put pen to paper and sat again on the same kitchen chair, transfixed in my pain as I wrote the words on the page, tears splashing the paper, dissolving my heartache into the words. It was a slow, quiet and lonely walk to the mailbox, and I waited for the sound of the envelope to land on top of the others. My face blank and my voice gone. As if in a trance, I wound my way back home and sat. It had been just one month since we all met and fell in love. Most relationships last longer than a month, but this love affair was doomed to end. In searching for my truth I fell into a well of untruths. How did this happen?

One person would know, and I needed to tell her what I'd done.

TELLING

Another benefit of living beyond visiting distance is voiceless conversations can take place by email without fear of a face-to-face confrontation. I could write and check and reflect before I hit 'send'.

3/2/2012 – Karen

Dear Ann, years back you gave me the name of my biological father as Silvio Ninni. You said that he had a girlfriend at the time of my conception and they went on to marry and have a son called Anthony. I also got the strong sense that this subject was a closed book and that information was all that you were willing to impart.

Late last year I wrote to Silvio. He and Maxine are the parents of Anthony (now 44) and Benjamin (34). Within a week of the letter being sent, I received an amicable phone call from Ben. We spoke at some length. He told me that Silvio and Maxine were shocked to hear of my existence, although no denial from Silvio that you and he had been involved. They both recall knowing of your pregnancy and of meeting David. Apparently there was an assumption that you were carrying David's baby. Nonetheless they took on board this new information, however did ask if I'd be interested in having a DNA test, to which I agreed.

Ben and I had a tentative arrangement to meet for a coffee when we were in Sydney in the New Year. At this meeting, at Café Gioia in Norton Street, Leichardt, Ben surprised me with Silvio and Maxine's presence. Maxine was very warm and expressed her understanding of my wanting to find my biological father, as she'd been on a similar path herself some years ago. Silvio expressed his shame and embarrassment, although did remain quiet throughout the meeting. We all asked and answered as many questions as we could. I heard that you had introduced Maxine to Silvio and that Maxine and you shared the same accommodation in Sydney – a place for country students and that your circle of friends was a lively bunch and that you and her enjoyed your nights out but were careful not to neglect your studies. She asked after you and your family and if you had finished pharmacology studies. Maxine gave me a photo of her and Silvio taken in 1964 in your backyard in Wrightson Avenue, which some time ago she had made into calling cards used for an overseas trip.

We all agreed that I would make the necessary arrangements for a DNA test, which I did through Silbase in Fitzroy, as referred by a friend of mine. We took the 'Peace of Mind' test.

Yesterday I received the results of this test, which revealed that Silvio Ninni is not my biological father.

Today I had an appointment with a counsellor, which provided a valuable opportunity to unravel this turn of events, including some unravelling of my emotions.

I can't really imagine how you will be receiving this news. Throughout this whole process I've been respectful of all involved. My respect for you is why this search has taken so long, however I could no longer ignore my desire and right to know the complete story of my paternity. I don't wish to cause you distress, and find myself in a difficult situation. However, now I need to ask you for more information. Who is my biological father?

Your understanding will be greatly appreciated.

4/2/2012 – Ann

I am very sorry that the results of the DNA test you arranged have disproved what I have always genuinely believed...

She regretted the unnecessary distress this has caused then went on to tell me that she would not be providing me with any other information because she couldn't remember the name of…

> the only other person – who used a condom – with whom I had sex before you were conceived.

5/2/2012 – Karen

I've always believed what you told me was what you believed to be true, which is why I can imagine this news will come as a shock for you as well. We've both been living with this information for such a long time. Whether I had met Silvio or not, his name and presence has loomed large in my life for many years, and that of my family.

From a very early age, around 8 years, I was told that my biological father was Italian. I need to know if this is still the case as Italian heritage has been a significant part of my identity. This is extremely important to me. While you may not recall the name of this other man, do you recall if he was of Italian heritage?

5/2/2012 – Ann

Yes – for what it's worth. I have not heard of/from him since the night in question and will not be providing you with any further information.

I was gutted. She then requested of me, out of courtesy, to notify Julie and Gionni that Silvio is not my biological father.

5/2/2012 – Karen

Thank you. All information regarding my heritage is worth a lot to me.

I will advise Julie and Gionni that Silvio is not my biological father.

6/2/2012 – Ann

Maxine and Silvio were estranged at the time of your conception. We did not have a sexual relationship when they were a couple. Silvio and I had been friends before he met Maxine, and he was very distressed that they were no longer together when he first impulsively drove to Newcastle on his own to see me.

She went on to tell me about the boarding house she lived in while pregnant with me, a mansion in Henrietta Street in Double Bay, where she met David. While Silvio and Maxine told me when they saw that Ann was pregnant they assumed the baby (me) was David's, Ann told a different story. Ann wrote that when she showed Silvio her pregnant belly he offered her money to go away, which she declined. The pregnancy was never mentioned again, and she never saw Silvio or Maxine ever again.

I booked a counselling session with a generic provider immediately, who was empathic, understanding and very interested. It was helpful to be in a room with someone who didn't know me – to cry and feel sad, angry and hurt without causing my loved ones to worry. She didn't have any experience with adoption, so I thought it would help to speak with an adoption-specific service based in Victoria. This counsellor was good in one way – they knew the Victorian system and were experienced in dealing with people who had been relinquished as babies. They also helped relinquishing mothers and had an interest in different perspectives. When I asked about the child's right to know their father, they had a lot less to say. Very little has been written on the subject and they saw an obvious resource gap in this area. It seemed like there were thousands more worthy and troubling situations they had to deal with, and I couldn't reconcile between screaming for attention and feeling empathy for people doing it much tougher than me.

I sent a text message to my brother Neil to let him know what I'd thought to be true was not. As I'd involved his family it was reasonable for me to pass on the news. I received a lacklustre text in response; maybe it was shock or maybe he thought I was an idiot for even trying. Maybe he was sorry I'd been hurt. Maybe he didn't have the words. What words were there?

∞

FOR THE FIRST TIME in my life, I was dreading my birthday. I hated it. I couldn't bring myself to make a plan or imagine what I'd do. A friend called me early in the day with her usual passion and vigour, full of song and cheer, wanting to know what I was doing in the evening. She could tell something was wrong – in minimal words I managed to tell her what had happened. She wanted to see me and insisted I tell her where I was having dinner that night. My brother-in-law joined us at a local pub and while I welcomed the distraction, I felt like shit, weighed down with shock and grief, unable to make small talk or ask anyone how they'd been.

There was an eerie silence around my birthday, not only due to the fact I had lost the ability to speak, through shock. My aunty, Bron, and my sister Madeline, were notably absent;

no pop-ins, texts or phone calls. In the beginning I was good with that, as I was mostly numb and without semblance of speech, but as the days went by, I started to layer the silence with imagined meaning. Eventually, a call came from Bron, but there was no 'Happy Birthday'. She was telling me plans had changed on the date for my cousin's farewell celebration, it was now postponed. My mind, barely operating on a parallel plane, my heart still bruised from the lightning strike a few weeks earlier, I met her words with caution.

'How was your birthday?' she asked.

'Not great, it's been a difficult time,' I tried to explain.

Without acknowledgement of my experience, she went on to say, 'It's been a terrible time for Ann, she's been very distressed and I heard her cry for the first time in my life.' I was being scolded for Ann's distress. And that was that.

16 February 2012

Dear Silvio and Maxine,

Thank you for your thoughtful letter and lovely birthday card, which I received on the 8 February. Although I am still quite saddened by recent events, our meeting, while under exceptional circumstances, I can see has been positive. I would like to think that while I may not have found family, my family and I may have well found some dear friends. Thank you again.

Since I last wrote to you I've managed to find out just a little more information that I wanted to share with you. I wrote to Ann with news of my meeting with you and subsequent test and results confirming that Silvio is not my biological father. Ann's initial response to me was that she was 'very sorry that the results of the DNA test you arranged have disproved what I have always genuinely believed, and regret the unnecessary distress that this will have caused to everyone concerned.' She continued... 'I will not be providing you with any further information of the only other person – who used a condom – with whom I had sex before you were conceived.'

It was a distressing reply; however, I acknowledge that this news would have been a huge shock – especially when her long-held belief had been now proven to be untrue. I reminded her that I had been told when I was eight years old that my father was Italian. I asked her if she could please tell me if that was still true. She did confirm that yes, this man was Italian.

Ann wrote shortly afterwards asking me to inform Julie & Gionni of the news that Silvio is not my biological father. I expect they have lived with this knowledge for over 47 years and that Ann wants to set that part of the record straight, if not the whole story.

As you may understand, my mind has been ticking over and over. Given what I know to date, I can't help but think that one of you, or both of you may be able to shed some light on any possibilities on who may be my biological father. This man of Italian origin would have been known to my mother Ann, and possibly your friends, specifically around May in 1964.

In one of Ann's emails to me, she wrote that at the time of my conception she was devastated to learn that Silvio's friend with whom she'd been smitten for a very long time and with whom she had been going out since they first met, had been telling Silvio's some untruths, in that he and Ann had had a sexual relationship.

I'm wondering if this man she refers to is Frank, the man she told me about, many years ago. I also can't help wonder if Frank could possibly be my biological father.

Since last October, my search has taken me on an intense journey of discovery. Many doors began to open for me and more recently it has felt like even larger doors have closed on top of me. I never knew when this search began, long ago, where it may lead. It is a chance I needed to take while being mindful to tread softly, softly to minimise impact and heartache for all concerned. I believe you understand my need and right to know of my parentage, and while I feel that you and your family have offered me a great deal already, I now need to go out on a limb and ask of you… If you have any details, thoughts or suggestions on the identity of my biological father, could you please let me know?

I realise you will be in preparation mode for Ben's wedding. What an exciting time for your family! I wish you all the very best in the lead up to the wedding and beyond, and I look forward to hearing from you. (We'd also love to see a wedding photo!)

With fondest regards, Karen

There was a silver lining to my dark cloud. I'd met some beautiful people, a family for whom I'd fallen head over heels. It was a fabulous consolation even though with every thought, letter, message and phone call I felt my loss with even greater intensity. They hadn't given up on me. The Ninnis had fallen for me and my darlings as well. They were deeply concerned for me. They had so many questions, but I did not have many answers. Time and time again I emphasised that Ann had truly believed Silvio was my father and that she'd been clearly shocked and very upset at the truth, proved scientifically by the DNA test. They have wondered to me often about who the other man might be and considered options. Frank had been counted out of the equation. They allowed me the opportunity to think aloud and ask questions of their youths in Sydney throughout 1964, about who was there, the names of clubs and restaurants, and especially the musicians. The Ninnis were still in contact with many of the old crew and they promised me they'd do what they could to keep thinking and asking on my behalf, if anyone out there knew the truth.

The truth is, as Ann would have it, that my biological father was the other guy – the guy who used the condom. He became 'condom man'. I was looking for Condom Man. 1964 was still the dawn of the sexual revolution and accessible contraception for women. Condoms were the most commonly used method to prevent a pregnancy, however they were not as easily available as they are today, and most certainly the onus was on the male to be prepared. Not many women would have been purchasing condoms in those days. I've imagined a man using a condom back then might have been cautious by nature, responsible at best and careful not to risk a pregnancy or scandal of any kind. Perhaps he was a man who had something to lose. I wasn't alone in my imaginings. It seemed that Andrew, the Ninnis and I started thinking along the same lines at around the same time.

Ann's best friend at the time, Julie, was newly married to an Italian man, Gionni. He used to manage the Swiss Club, a favoured supper club of the Italian and Australian crews who loved music, friendships and parties. Julie was studying medicine, very busy through the day, and Gionni worked at night. My thoughts led me to questioning whether Gionni could have had the means and opportunities to have had an affair with his new wife's best friend. I couldn't get this possibility out of my mind and when it was suggested by others, completely unprompted, it gave more power to my suspicions. This was completely feasible and might explain the falling out between the families. It could explain why Ann was so upset to learn that Silvio was not my father, that should the identity of 'Condom Man' be revealed as the husband of her best friend, it would be devastating to the way she was considered by others, and how she viewed herself.

The collective 'aha!' moment fuelled a fire within my camp and the Ninni camp. We couldn't let it go. Despite being in continual contact with the 'old crew,' the Ninnis had had nothing to do with Gionni and Julie over the years. Their only connection was the godfather to their son was also godfather to Julie and Gionni's son. Godfather Vittorio, or 'Vic' could hold the key.

I told Maxine about the letter I'd written Julie and Gionni more than a decade ago with the news of my first pregnancy, and my request to pass on the letter to Silvio, the man who Ann had named as my father. Both Maxine and Silvio knew I'd never heard from them since, and of my two guesses – that they either never received my letter, or that they did receive it and chose not to reply. The Ninnis told me that Vic remembers Julie and Gionni receiving the letter, and he had told Silvio at that time that there was a young woman trying to find him. My research tells me there was little else said at the time by anyone, and my letter of request had been swept under the carpet by Julie and Gionni, and also by Vic and by Silvio.

It was time to honour Ann's request and inform her old best friend Julie and her husband Gionni that the tests had revealed that Silvio was not my father, as she had always believed and as she'd told them all those years ago. Ann wanted me to tell them. While it was curious that Ann wouldn't contact Julie herself, I excused this with the idea that she did not want to enter into any conversation with Julie after so many years of estrangement, that she was in fact directing me to engage with people who might be able to provide me answers, rather than getting involved. Could it be that Ann didn't want to name him herself?

On 16 February 2012, I wrote to Julie and Gionni, reintroducing myself to them in a way, and bringing them up to speed with the events in my life over the years since my last letter, especially my children, my work, my volunteer work and studies. Naturally I enquired about their wellbeing and their family, particularly Joanna. I described how the past few months had taken me on a journey of discovery as I picked up the search for my biological father. I explained that for a long time I'd put the concerns and feelings for others ahead of my own, but the time had come for me to follow through on what I could no longer ignore.

I wanted them to understand the importance of family to me and that it was the many heartfelt conversations with my children that influenced me to pick up my search.

Gently I approached the topic of Ann and the recent series of heart-wrenching events which now posed more questions. I needed their help. I told them that Ann suggested I contact them, that she was eager for them to know that 'the man I thought to be your biological father has been proven otherwise'.

The crux of the letter was to let them know that Ann had decided she wouldn't provide me with any more information other than to confirm the only other person with whom she had sex before I was conceived had used a condom, and he was Italian. Her response had led to much speculation, and though

I was unsure of how Julie or Gionni would receive this news, and whether or not it would be of much interest or not, it did lead me to pose most pertinent questions: could either of them know anything that could bring me closer to learning the truth of my paternity? Could either of them know of an Italian man who Ann may have had a physical relationship/encounter with around May of 1964?

I appealed to Julie's particular interest in medicine and genetics and hoped she understood that the gap in my biological history was of additional importance.

Again, I received no response to my letter. Again, I thought this rather odd, not only because I'd written another letter, but I'd imagined their responses could have been either: 'Good to hear from you, sorry to hear that, we don't know anything, good luck,' or, 'Good to hear from you, sorry to hear that, we have some information that could help.'

Either response would've been understandable and gratefully received, but this silence? This no-reply pattern? It didn't make sense. I felt it was rude, and in some ways an admission of some knowledge which made them unable to respond.

Many months passed and I became Facebook friends with their daughter. Joanna and I had met the day Andrew and I arrived at her parent's place, and shared afternoon tea during that pivotal exchange of information and history. I sent her a message to see how she'd been going and enquiring how her family was. By now I wondered whether there had been some shock or illness in the family, and was genuinely interested in how everyone was doing. For all I knew, perhaps Julie and/or Gionni had died!

Somebody *had* died. Julie's mother, who had lived with them for many years had passed away around the time I had sent my letter, naturally a time of great sadness to the family. In a curious way, it gave me hope they weren't deliberately ignoring me, they were caught in the midst of emotional turmoil and grief.

A big piece of my picture was still missing, and I felt empty. In the throes of searching for my Italian identity I found myself weaving in and out of a tangled web of secrets and half-truths. I've had successes and absolute heartbreak that has at times impacted my ability to work and study and maintain relationships. It's severely compromised my relationship with my birth mother and her family. Yet no matter how much pain this search has caused, I feel driven and determined to pursue the search for my complete identity, which I believe is tied up with my ancestral knowledge.

18/3/12 – Karen

Dear Ann,

How are you? I've been thinking about how you are for weeks now and how, after the initial shock of the revelation about my paternity, you are feeling. I hope you have had a confidante in this time.

It's probably beyond time that I caught you up with where things have been for me and my family since the flurry of emails a few weeks back.

I sent a letter to Julie and Gionni on 17 February and have had no acknowledgement from them. I had thought a response of some sort was a reasonable expectation and wonder why you aren't able to contact Julie yourself? I have no idea why you have not been in touch for so many years, something I pondered 15/16 years ago when I contacted her myself. Clearly you both had been tremendous friends and had shared such significant times together.

Silvio and Maxine, while they have been through quite a lot in the past few months, do not seem to be holding any ill will toward anyone, however have an interest in the wellbeing of me and my family. They, and their family, were all captivated by the Ingrams, when we shared a lunch back in January. In my initial letter to you where I stated the facts of the past few months, I didn't emphasise the fact that Andrew, Angus and Brigit have been part of this whole journey as well and were very excited to be meeting, what we all thought, to be my biological father, and the children's grandfather. Their meeting with Silvio, Maxine and Ben was an amazing experience for all concerned. There was genuine rapport, which was also echoed in a lovely letter/card we received from Maxine just a week later, with an accompanying photograph of us all, taken by the waiter in the restaurant. Ben and I got along famously, Angus and Andrew had an incredible connection with him, and Silvio's face lit up when he met the children.

When we returned to Melbourne, everything in my home looked and felt completely different. I was excited, elated and complete. It had been an incredible journey where door after door was opened. I shared my story with several close friends and members of Andrew's family.

I've also not discussed any part of this 'journey' with my parents. They, and especially Mum, have become more and more sensitive around the topic of my adoption, and I believed, at the time, that I would not involve them and confuse a Christmas family reunion with the emotions surrounding another kind of family reunion. I wanted to, and succeeded at, giving them my undivided attention during our time in Newcastle. I also didn't know how everything would turn out, after meeting Silvio. I made every effort to respect the feelings of all concerned while fulfilling my own needs to fill the big gap in my life, my heart and my future. I did however, tell my brother Neil, as we were staying with him and his family in Sydney throughout this 'leg of the tour.'

I truly appreciated your symbolic gesture of sending me the Swarovski angel wing twin pendants however your request to send one of them on to my mother presented a complex circumstance. Initially I tried hard to reconcile your request and finally I decided that your kind gesture would be best left between you and I. You mentioned at the time that you weren't able to send a card with the gift. I wonder, if you could have sent a card, what would you have said? After much reflection, I would like to share this gift with Brigit, to be given to her at some point in the future, knowing that it is a gift from you, to me, to her – down the maternal line.

This whole series of events has brought about much sadness, grief, loss and uncertainty. I truly fell in love with the Ninnis. I would never have put my children in a situation to do the same if I believed there to be any doubt. It was a truly believable and credible story. I do not blame you for giving me this information about Silvio and can completely understand why you believed him to be my father. I'll continue to work through what I need to recover from this shock, however for me, it is not over. It is something I will live with every day. For some time now, I've been drawn to explore identity. I'm surrounded by identity issues at work, in my studies and in everyday conversation with my family, friends and colleagues. Identity is important, and I would say especially important to adopted children. For others, I would say biological identity can be taken for granted.

While you cannot remember the name of this other man, can you tell me anything about the circumstances in which you met him? What do you remember about him? Was he a friend/relative of one of your friends? Would anyone else be able to recall his name? I wonder if his identity, or lack thereof, gives reason as to why I haven't received a reply from Julie or Gionni? Perhaps they may know something, yet don't feel like they have permission to speak up? As you can see, without any other details about my biological father, other than he was an Italian man who wore a condom, my ponderings continue.

I really hope you can understand my need for more information. My emotional and physical health has been compromised in these past weeks – I'm well aware of the connection between emotional pain and ill health. From the day I received the DNA results I have an acute flare up of my pre-existing bowel condition and associated symptoms, not to mention insomnia. My health is one motivator to obtain clarity and resolve. Of course my children are another.

With love,

Karen

18/3/12 – Ann

A card from me for your mother would include the following variation on the verse by that prolific author, Anonymous – the original of which is usually for adoptees and which I know your mother has given you.

NOT FLESH OF YOUR FLESH, NOR BONE OF YOUR BONE
BUT STILL MIRACULOUSLY YOUR OWN,
PLEASE DON'T FORGET, FOR EVEN A MINUTE
SHE DID NOT GROW UNDER YOUR HEART, BUT IN IT.

I sent Angus an email this afternoon to ask about his milestone birthday on Friday.

She reiterated, again, that she would not be providing me with any further information and further wrote…

> Conception still occurs in ignorance, apathy, anger and error – as well as love – and many people, including you, will never know their biological father.
>
> I will regret until my dying day that I ever gave you (in good faith and against my better judgement) Silvio Ninni's name, but each of us is responsible for our own choices/actions and the ramifications thereof – however painful.

I had no words. I was empty. Flattened. I could not reply.

In January, the month before the earth fell away, when I was still full of hope and positivity, I was excited to receive a fantastic email from my aunt Prudence, who revealed some family history that I found fascinating. By chance and lucky coincidence, she'd come across some familial relics that belonged to her father, Old Jim. I shared her excitement and replied that I'd love to know more, as it was really very important for me to get to know my family folklore, piecing together the puzzled past. She told me she'd get back to me after the school holidays because she'd be busy looking after her grandkids. Apart from Prudence it was only my sister and me who expressed interested in our family history, and her email was like gold to me. I couldn't wait for more news.

I was engulfed in silence. My several emails to Prudence bounced back, undelivered. I kept trying because I trusted our connection and the bond we'd shared since our first meeting and subsequent family catch-ups over the years, in Newcastle, in Melbourne, and in Tasmania. I reread her words to me over these years, confident in their sincerity. But now, something had shifted. Feeling the earth beneath me cracking apart, I had to face the reality that she had no intention of replying. I tried hard to let it be. Despite the cracks beneath me, I got on with my abundant life, my studies, my work and loving my family.

Eventually, after my voice had returned, I started telling my story to people I trusted – I couldn't have handled cross-examinations or a flippant, 'Oh well.' I wanted to tell my story without judgement, with some sense of understanding. The man I thought was my father is not. The woman who is my birth mother is refusing to give me any more information. The book is closed. The end. She said so. The end.

Each time someone asked about Ann and my family the painful truth resurfaced. Further enamoured by my favourite season through March to May, I tried to shed my expectations, the hopes I once had, and the great, deep sadness inside. Colours around me were changing, what had become so strikingly emblazoned with intensity from January, now the normally vibrant autumn palette had become muted. Leaves fell like my tears and my expectations drifted toward the big freeze of winter. The big freeze. I had been frozen in shock. Frozen out. Contact with my family, frozen. Chilled to the bone, chilled to my core. They were no longer interested in me or my perspective.

SYDNEY, ART AND GHOSTS FROM THE PAST

It was November 2013 when Maxine sent me the details of her exhibition. Her paintings, which I'd greatly admired through photos she'd sent to my phone, were inspired by nature. I'd told her many times how I'd love to see them in person one day. She'd been feverishly working on many more artworks in readiness for a solo exhibition. I didn't know how I was going to get there. It would've been a financial and logistical wrench to manage the four of us 'popping up' to Sydney for a couple of days. Whether driving or flying, I couldn't see how it could happen. Money was tight. As time ticked on, I became increasingly overwhelmed by a sense of urgency, and that somehow I must get to Sydney to attend the opening of Maxine's exhibition – she had hinted at all the people she wanted me to meet. So I booked a flight.

My head was crowded with thoughts and possibilities of what may lie ahead. As soon as I grasped each thought I tried hard to release it, to let it slip into the ether. I was heading towards something that I had no control over. All I could do was treat myself, and others, with kindness and respect. I was truly excited about seeing Maxine's paintings in real life, on a gallery wall, among her people, in celebration. I couldn't wait.

Somewhere during the train and bus trip from Mascot to Glebe, I called the Post Adoption Resource Centre – the very place that had linked me with Ann so many years before. I was hoping for a counselling appointment before the exhibition later in the evening, however their change of location to the outer-west mucked up those plans. Instead I booked an appointment for the next day, en route to the airport and my trip home.

With a few hours to spare before the exhibition I wandered up to Broadway, soaking up the sights, smells and sounds of Sydney, my Sydney, the city to which no other could hold a beacon. I'd romanticised her from childhood, through adolescence, boyfriends, bands, friends and parties well into my adulthood; and she still excited me. Aimlessly wandering, I came to a nail bar and treated myself to a manicure, for an improvement to my petite, stubby, soft and bendy nails that had always let me down. I know the women in nail bars try and hide their horror or surprise upon first sight of my nails. I can tell their change of expression behind their masks, some hide it better than others. Some may comment, 'Ooh, they are so cute – so tiny!' at best. I chose a light green polish, and was pleased with the result.

After, I gave the taxi driver the address of the gallery, and enjoyed the inner-urban scenery as the taxi meandered its way around the streets. It was great to get off Parramatta Road and see more of my city of Sydney. The red-brick homes spanning three centuries, the terracotta-tiled roofs and the steps from curb to stoop. Every turn, ascent and descent brought about a feeling of entering into a familiar, yet unknown place. I didn't know how far we had to go or how much the fare would be, and was unprepared for the stop. I'd been distracting myself from the enormity of what might happen, who I might meet, by daydreaming out the window, watching the houses and street signs.

My breathing was shallow, palms sweating, and my stomach was bouncing against my diaphragm. 'You're one gutsy woman, Karen,' I assured myself, knowing full well that I was about to walk into a room full of people, most of whom were unknown to me. Making my way for the door, I walked past a handful of lingering smokers in jovial conversation on the footpath. My focus was on greeting Maxine and Silvio and viewing the artwork. And having a drink. And a bite to eat – no, way too nervous to eat. The sound of a hundred people chattering became louder and louder as I approached the doorway. I entered. The gallery was stuffed with people, from wall to wall to wall to wall. I was immensely reassured; in a room like this I could be invisible. That feeling soon abated, as I didn't come all this way to be invisible. I wanted to be seen. I wanted to be present and in the space, for anyone to see.

I noticed Maxine almost immediately but it took several minutes to weave in and around others to reach her. She looked absolutely splendid and completely in her element at the opening night of her solo art exhibition. I was thrilled for her. She saw me in her periphery, her eyes lit with joy and love, and she took my hand and drew me close. We hugged and she thanked me so much for coming. I was excitedly at ease. Silvio wasn't far away and seeing him for the first time since the

DNA results hit me harder than I imagined. He was so happy to see me, and we held hands as we kissed each other's cheeks, tears welling from my heart to my eyes. I pulled it together just as Maxine took my hand telling me, 'I have some people you must meet.'

She took me around the gallery introducing me to countless people, all knew my story, or at least the part where it intersected with the lives of Silvio and Maxine. While I was warmly greeting strangers, they were responding with firm hand-holding and long looks into my eyes. They exchanged looks with Maxine. One woman told me, 'You mean a great deal to Silvio and Maxine.' Another took my hand as she said, 'Karen, Maxine has told me so much about you.'

Silvio and Maxine guided me to a group of older Italian men and a couple of women – wives of the men. They introduced me in Italian as Ann's daughter. I watched their expressions change as years flashed before their eyes. They all looked at me, up and down, into my eyes, studying my face and my manner. They stood there somewhat shocked as I stood before them as some kind of ghost from the past. I look so much like Ann; a friend they hadn't seen for almost fifty years. A conversation swirled around me, in Italian. As Maxine introduced me some of the men's names were familiar – especially Frank and Vic. These two, and Silvio, were names Ann had mentioned to me many years before. Of course, they remembered Ann. One of them took my hand and leaned towards me.

'Your mother, she was so beautiful. You look just like her.' I was filled with love, pride and sadness at once. Words escaped me.

Everyone was so gracious and interested in me. Silvio introduced me to a female friend and she took my hand, looked into my eyes and said, 'Oh Karen, it's so lovely to meet you. You do know how much Silvio wishes you were his daughter.'

I wept deep inside, and suppressed my heart, which wanted to jump into the room and around them all. A tear rolled down my cheek and I looked at Silvio, his eyes were twinkling with tears. He asked if I'd like to go outside to talk, it was very noisy in the gallery.

Together Silvio and I sat on the brick fence of the house next door to the gallery. He wanted to help me, and he still had more questions. He was certain that somebody knew something, and again wondered why Ann was being so secretive, 'Why would she put my name out there yet refuse to give the name of the other man, the one who used a condom?' Then he told me, 'I think I know who it is, Karen. It must be Gionni.'

He asked me to make contact with Gionni and I told him I had received no reply to my letter informing him and his wife Julie of the outcomes of the DNA test. Silvio insisted, 'You should ask Gionni directly.'

Back in the gallery the sounds of the chatter had gone up a few decibels. I was well and truly ready for a wine so made a dash to the bar, which is when I saw Ben. I can barely say his name without recalling his passion, excitement and enthusiasm from the time we first spoke on the phone, to our first meeting and the phone call following the revelation of the DNA results. It was wonderful to see him, he'd been married in the meantime and I was keen to meet his beautiful wife, who sadly wasn't there. We talked for some time about many things. My internal dialogue was echoing the words of Silvio's friend from earlier and I found myself wishing for the truth to be Silvio, instantly realising that pretending and wishing was neither real nor true. Conscious of the fact I hadn't looked at Maxine's paintings I made my way back to the gallery walls and was taken aback further by the enormity of my friend's artistic and soulful spirit, evident in her work on the walls, but also the people she drew into the space. The energy was electric.

I became aware of people looking at me and talking about me, mostly in Italian and obviously not inviting me to join in. I let them look. I let them soak my presence in. I was Ann's daughter, the daughter of a woman they had known as their friend. Frank asked me, 'How is Ann? Where is she living now?' I gave a respectful and courteous reply. I told him she is well and living in Tasmania. He asked if she married and had other children and I told him she had. Honestly, I didn't know how she was because she'd shut me out.

'I was very fond of Ann when we were young,' he said.

Words spoken and whispered, glances exchanged, stares directed toward me. I can never know what they meant or what knowledge and memories they held, which could lift the lid on my truth. As Silvio said, somebody must know something and, as Ben had told me, if those Italians don't want me to know, they will clam shut and there's no way I'll know anything. That was hard to hear and harder to digest. Bastards. If you know something, say something!

Ben and I found each other again as we made our way

around the gallery walls. Suddenly I remembered he had a brother! I asked if Tony was there and, although I was aware of his disdain for me and my sudden appearance in the lives of his family, I was still very interested in meeting him. A part of me thought that if he met me in person he would see that I'm no threat, especially as his parents and brother were welcoming of me. I quickly checked in with Ben, 'Are you sure it will be ok for me to meet him?' He was certain it would be fine and pointed him out. I walked towards him and we made eye contact. I smiled and reached out my hand and said

'Hello Tony, I'm Karen.'

He was gracious enough to shake my hand, briefly, said hello and then walked away. It was very clear he was not okay about meeting me and most likely unhappy that I was there. I let it go instantly. He was gone.

Later that night, as my head touched the pillow, I tried to still my mind; I reflected on what had occurred, in a series of thoughts and sounds:

I GLIDED INTO THE gallery, my feet barely touching the floor yet firmly planted on the ground. Like a ghost from a past life lost, I appeared before them. I am here. More than a story to be told over coffee, I am here, fully present before you, a touchable mirage sparking memories and stories – so many stories. When my story began you were young adults, brimming with vigour, with ideas you carried from your old country to your new. You arrived here to make a life for yourself, to live your life to the fullest, squeezing every drop from the vine into your bucket, gathering love, friendships and stories along the way. I am part of that story. We are connected. Lift the lid on the box you closed long ago.

My head and heart were both spinning wildly in a whirly wind of emotions – my head back, arms out and toes together. I'd gathered the energy of the gallery, zeroed in on several clusters and placed myself in the midst of an unchartered galaxy. I allowed myself to be carried away in the energy, imagining that something would come of it – new information would emerge and the melting permafrost of these men's minds would reveal a telling, leading to my truth.

∞

MY OVERNIGHT BAG WAS packed and placed by the door; I sat face-to-face with a new character, Natalie, a counsellor who sat quietly and attentively as she listened to my story unfold. She was perfect. Allowing me time to start, stop and start again, she asked the right questions at the right times. She was captivated. As the tissue mound grew in the bin beside me, we started working on strategies to keep me going. I always felt better when I knew there was something else I could do, when I was ready, a next step. I felt better with hope. The time had come to connect with Gionni directly. I needed to know if he was my biological father and, more importantly, if he would take a DNA test.

Realising that a scientific test was the only marker I could trust, I needed to somehow arrive at this point with a man who I had met only once, and who had been silent towards me for many years. Natalie made the contact with Gionni by registered post in a letter requesting he phone her. The letter explained that she had met me and that we needed his assistance. Within a week of the letter being delivered Natalie received a phone call from Julie. She called to explain that Gionni had received the letter however he was unable to use the telephone due to his significant deafness. She was able to get messages to him. It was confirmed that Gionni was sitting next to her while the phone call was taking place. Julie took the next step, reading between the lines of the short letter, and assuring Natalie that Gionni was not my biological father. This confusing exchange left me with more questions than answers due to the absence of Gionni's voice. Julie was a medical doctor and currently was listed as a genetic counsellor. My suspicions became heightened. Something wasn't quite right.

It was during this phone call with Natalie that Julie advised that Gionni would be willing to do a DNA test. Then she dropped a new name into the mix. She and Gionni recalled there was another musician in the band who they believe had been friendly with Ann. They described him as a session musician, filling in on guitar for a while before moving on – to where, they didn't know. His name: Giovanni Ficca.

This latest account had me in a further tailspin. How much of what Julie said could be trusted? The new name was either a red herring or a potential contender for the title of Condom Man, or both. I couldn't dismiss it, yet I still had to address the question of Gionni. I could only manage one contender at a time. I needed to contact Gionni directly, and was bothered that he was unable to make phone calls due to his hearing loss. It didn't sit well with me. I'd spent the past months searching for the courage I needed to reach out directly to Gionni. I needed to do something. One day, having drawn the elusive courage from thin air, I psyched myself up to make a phone call. It rang out. No answering machine, no clues, nothing. I hung up. Hoping the courage I mustered that day would find me again, I left it there and mulled over what everything meant.

I revisited the conversation between Natalie and Julie. Within days I found myself facing the phone on the bookshelf, willing it into my hand and searching for the courage of heart to try again. Bingo. Gionni answered the phone and we spoke for some time. His hearing seemed perfectly fine to me which had me guessing about the authenticity of the earlier claim by Julie. As Gionni and I spoke, I walked around the lounge room, stopping occasionally to perch on a chair, write some things down and rise again, searching for the horizon from my rear window. What I couldn't see, I imagined; Gionni's face and hands and the time and distance between us. He was absolutely lovely. He spoke to me with love and concern. He told me with all honesty that he and Ann never had an affair – and they didn't even kiss on the lips. He told me that he wished it was true, he wished I was his daughter and then I would know. He told me that his daughter Joanna had cried tears for me and my story, and that I had a strong ally in her. He told me he would take a DNA test, hearing my plea for proof. I'd been hurt so deeply before – he could tell in my voice. I proposed to him that Joanna could assist him with the DNA test, so as not to inconvenience (or provoke) Julie. He agreed.

Then he spoke of Giovanni. All he had was a name and a recollection he would have been on the scene in 1964. The time of my conception was May, yet he could not be so specific about the time. Giovanni was passing through, he said. He stayed for a few months – maybe he went travelling afterwards. Now I had two possibilities and next steps to work on in my own time. The thing is, my time is precious, and people are getting older; while my heart and head need to be ready to take any steps, I couldn't afford to be idle for long.

That night I spoke with Joanna on the phone. She was of enormous support and wholeheartedly agreed with my proposal to have a DNA kit to be sent in her father's name to her address. She took it to him and was there when he took his saliva sample with the cotton swab, and put it in the tube. They posted it to the lab in Melbourne. I sat in the same spot on the side of my bed as I had the first time I'd done a test. So much had happened since then, so much hope and love lost. I sealed the envelope and walked around the corner to the same mailbox where I'd dropped off other life-changing letters. The sound of a soft thud as it hit the mail already there reassured me that I hadn't missed the collection. Then I waited.

Not long after I received a letter in the mail. I paused before I opened it. I could no longer trust my own instincts as far as this was concerned. I just needed the proof, so that my heart could heal and hopefully open once again. The notice revealed a myriad of numbers in columns, and finally words that confirmed that Gionni was NOT my father. It was the last three words that affected me the greatest. Memories of the trauma I encountered the first time around hit me again. My head was pragmatic in its response – rationalising the benefits of a process by elimination. It wasn't Gionni – let's move on. My heart took a little longer to catch up, but it did.

The good news was I did have a next step to take. I had another name. He could be absolutely anywhere. So I took to Google and the white pages and a few other searching methods. I found two listings for G Ficca in Australia. Joanna had recently sent a photo of Ann she had found in her parents' albums – taken before I was born, before she was pregnant with me. I decided to include the image in the letter.

Dear Mr Ficca,

I am looking for someone who could be important to me and am hoping you may be able to help.

His name is Giovanni Ficca and he would have spent time in Sydney Australia in 1964. We understand he was a musician at that time and played in a band with some other Italians, including the Swiss Club or the Mandalay in Lane Cove. He knew my friend's father Gionni who managed the club and spent some time with the woman in the picture, her name is Ann. He may have been in his 20s which would mean he would be a man of 70 years or more at present. We think he may have returned to Italy after his time in Sydney.

Could this man I describe, Giovanni Ficca, be a member of your family in Australia or Italy, or even another country? If so, could you please let me know his contact details and/or forward my letter on to him?

My letter is genuine and is sent with utmost discretion and respect. I mean no harm. If you or anyone you know may have any information that could help, please let me know.

Yours sincerely, Karen Ingram

Within a week of sending the letter I woke one morning, got out of bed and got to my mobile phone, which had been charging in the kitchen overnight. There was a missed call from an unknown number at 6.15am. No message. I was rushing to an appointment in the city and didn't give it too much thought. I didn't hear my phone ring again over the din of the city streets and I went straight into my meeting. Checking my phone while walking up Swanston Street, I noticed there had been another call from the same number, and this time they'd left a message. I tried hard to hear the message with so much background noise. Finding a quiet spot to sit, the foyer of the Ian Potter Gallery at Federation Square, I heard as much of the message as I was able. It was a man with a very thick Italian accent.

He received my letter late yesterday and could not stop thinking about it. He could tell that I was very genuine and understood my need to know and search for my father. The G Ficca at his address was in fact his wife's name – sadly he was not Giovanni Ficca. However, his brother is Giovanni Ficca. He lived in Geelong, and the two brothers spoke of my letter the night before. He wanted to call me to let me know that they did not arrive in Australia until in 1967, two years after I was born.

There was no way that this man's brother could be my father. I sat on a stool surrounded by pigeons outside a cafe at Fed Square and wept as Mr Ficca, a stranger, expressed interest and concern for me. He understood my need to know. This man showed me more compassion and understanding than the biological family I knew. It made me weep harder. As the moments stood still, I pressed the phone hard against my ear, hanging onto Mr Ficca's every word, I was only aware of the pigeons on the ground. I couldn't look up. My head was bowed, shoulders hunched and my arm taut. I thanked him with all my heart, and with my expression of gratitude. I wept even more and I hung up. What a beautiful man, who cared so deeply about the search of a stranger, of me, that it kept him awake last night, and compelled him to call me first thing this morning. Twice! I won't forget it.

Reality was sinking in. Finding an Italian man who played guitar and who happened to be in Sydney in 1964 was a long shot. He could be anywhere in the world. He could be dead. I realised how many clues I had when searching for Silvio. This search could take forever, and I didn't have forever to find him. A long-lost friend I'd been reacquainted with was travelling around Italy visiting family and on a late-night whim, I sent him a message to ask if he could look up the phone book where he was and see if there were any Giovanni Ficca's listed. He was just heading out for the day with his cousin and happily obliged. Within hours I had two Italian addresses for Giovanni Ficca. My wonderful ally Joanna agreed to translate the letters for me, and to be the Italian speaking contact for a reply. Again, I followed my previous footsteps to the mailbox around the corner, dropping two more letters, registered post, to Italy. I received notice that one of the letters reached its destination. That is all.

SEEKING MY TRUTH

The longing and yearning for my familial roots continued to run deep. Deeply hurt from the communication freeze by Ann and her sisters, I was left in a position of unknowing. I kept thinking about Nana and how she was doing. The letter I'd sent her at Christmas was returned to sender. I wondered if she too was subject to a command of the communication freeze. The last I heard she'd had a fall at home and been moved to more appropriate housing close by in the Hunter Valley. Knowing little else, my thoughts turned to the worst-case scenario. Perhaps she'd died. The continual loss was heartbreaking. Each time I had a thought or a question I relived the utter sadness of having nowhere to place it. I was isolated with deep pain in my heart.

I contacted my cousin Emma; even though we hadn't seen each other for many years, I hoped our connection from when we met in Tasmania and in sporadic moments since would still ring true. In my message I asked after our Nana, and if she had a current address, as I really wanted to make contact to let her know I was thinking about her. I had absolutely no intention or desire to bleed my heart all over her. She replied that her mum, my aunt Barbara, would be happy for me to make contact with Nana, with the caveat that I not mention anything to do with Ann. I happily agreed to the conditions, and was thrilled to hear that Nana was indeed still alive and now living in an aged care facility in Forster, New South Wales. Somehow a letter to her seemed almost impossible to write. I needed to see her.

It was Easter and we'd planned a family trip to Newcastle. It was to be a special time that involved a road trip, staying at my brother's place and visiting Mum and Dad with a special lunch on Easter Sunday. Anzac Day was upon us and the new Anzac Memorial Walk – a boardwalk along some of Newcastle's cliff tops, from Strzelecki Lookout to Bar Beach, the cliff tops of my childhood dreams – was to be opened to the public for the first time on the 25th of April. Two days before, we gave ourselves a preview by passing through the construction tape and sliding between a gap in the cyclone fencing. I was reunited with the vistas of my beloved cliff tops and rooftops, sea spray and ocean-lined horizon of Awabakal country and the waters beyond. It was the closest I could come to hang-gliding over the views that had captivated my waking and sleeping life. I could almost see the rooftop and backyard of the house in Wrightson Avenue, where Ann lived with her family before she moved to Sydney. We stepped out onto the high pathway, stopping to reflect on the names of local soldiers etched into striking sculpted figures. Of course, others who had busted through the tape gravitated to the family names, recalling stories and folklore of great-grandfathers, grandfathers and uncles who went to war. Like another hit to the face, I became anxious as I flailed around trying to find a family name. I wasn't even sure whose name I was looking for. In the end I settled with the thought that it couldn't matter for me if any of these men were my forebears – in truth they were somebody's, and that was enough.

My relationship with memorialising our casualties of war, and those injured and suffering, is complex. My heart aches for their sacrifice, and that of the women and children these soldiers left behind. And those who returned and their families, who faced the cold, hard reality that their loved one was a permanently changed man, often with undiagnosed nor recognised trauma or illness. I will never celebrate it, but I will commemorate them, with a strong sense of futility. We continue to make the same mistakes that result in conflict, which reduce the lives of defence forces and civilians to political fodder.

I reserved a day out of our holiday schedule to take a long road trip to visit Nana in her new home, a considerable distance from where she lived previously. With my darlings beside me, I headed to a place I hadn't visited since I was a child. Excited and trepidatious, we set off on an adventure to a path unknown. This trip was much more than 'a visit to Nana'. We navigated our way north, filled with wonder and the promise that we would return to this part of the coast again one day. The subtropical sights delighted us, and as we got closer we firmed up our plans. I would visit Nana first for about half an hour and then Andrew and the kids would come in – a familiar scenario.

Cautiously, I stepped into the corridor of the home and

found my way to Nana's room. There she was. Slight of frame and obviously fragile, she was sitting on top of her bed, fully dressed, looking out a window. I walked in carefully holding a bunch of flowers I'd bought from the shopping centre down the road.

'Nana – hello, it's me, Karen.'

Thankfully my aunt had given Nana a heads-up I was visiting. Her face lit up like a moonbeam, she looked beautiful as she beckoned me closer with her stellar smile and kind voice.

We sat together as she willingly responded to my many questions. I told her I wanted to know more about her and her life, and our family history, which I was so very interested in. She told me many things. When I asked her what Old Jim was like she replied with more than a hint of disdain, 'He was a difficult man.' She told me of her unrealised dreams as a young woman to continue her studies, to become a teacher. She was a child of the Great Depression, an era particularly hard for women and young girls, who, by today's standards, never had a hope of realising their dreams beyond domesticity and motherhood. Nana worked as domestic help for a family in a regional town in central New South Wales. Her daily errands included a visit to the chemist, which is where she met Old Jim, almost twenty years her senior. He took a great liking to her and they began courting under the watchful eye of her disapproving sister.

I talked to Nana a little bit about my work and my passion for Aboriginal affairs, health and education, and ultimately social justice, which I'm so proud to say she shared with me – she understood. I pondered aloud with her why I had kept returning to the sphere of Aboriginal Australia and then I asked, 'Is there any chance there could be Aboriginal heritage in our family?' It was a long shot but nonetheless an increasingly nagging question I needed to ask. I'm sure she'd never been asked it before. She told me she didn't know for sure, and if there had been it most likely wouldn't have been disclosed or discussed. Then she recalled a story her grandmother had told her, about her early years living deep in the bushland of the Hunter Valley, behind the town of Scone, in a place called Sparkes Creek. It was very isolated, and they lived in a makeshift shanty-style house where they raised their children. Neighbouring families dotted the remote landscape and they stood together through tough times. It was the time of the gold rush and the men had left to go south and try their luck, leaving the women and children behind. Her story went on to describe the bushranger gangs who travelled and thieved their way through remote areas, avoiding the force of colonial law. On several occasions, Aboriginal men in the area would sense danger and give advance warning to Nana's grandmother so she could be prepared to either hide or have a meal ready, as an offering in order to avoid any physical danger.

I have craved family folklore all my life. The stories of my grandparents and parents that I absorbed as my own, creating vivid images in my mind at every telling. This story that Nana told me only once will stay with me forever.

We talked some more, and discovered something new that we had in common. I was stoked and surprised to find out we both went to Cardiff Primary School, the same school my brothers and Dad attended. I had no idea that Nana used to live in Cardiff – an important detail that somehow had eluded me all of these years. My great-grandfather built their house in Oxley Parade, which intersected with the street my Mumma and Poppa lived on. Nana was about ten years older than my dad so it's unlikely they ever crossed paths in the neighbourhood. This was wonderful news. As a child I had unknowingly trodden the same footpaths, corridors and steps that my biological maternal grandmother had. Paired with the knowledge that I had also trod the same footsteps as my birth mother, Ann, during high school, this was a beautiful, strong connection that I had with these women. I felt fortunate to have discovered this in my time with Nana that day.

She thanked me for visiting and I really felt I sparked her mind, not only recalling memories in response to my questions, but giving us the chance to get to know each other – as wondering, questioning women with a connection.

We had driven a long way to see Nana and it was time to say goodbye. I had so many more questions and I was sure that was my last chance to ask them. I wanted our goodbye to be beautiful, but it in the end it was just sad. It's unlikely I'll ever see her again. I took her frail hand in mine, leaned in and gently kissed her soft cheek,

'I'm so glad I came to visit Nana, we'll see you soon.'

INTERRUPTED

After the abrupt end to my email correspondence with Ann in May (2012), I heard nothing from her until a large package arrived days before Christmas. It came with no message, card or letter – which was not unusual. I unwrapped the layers of packaging to reveal a nativity set of ceramic tea light candle holders. We were heading north to spend Christmas with my family, so I hurriedly unpacked them and added them to our front window display. It was a lovely yet cumbersome gift, which spoke volumes about Ann, her love of nativity sets and her innate ability to source items and arrange for their delivery. She didn't drive, and was a late adopter of the internet, so it was no mean feat.

Birthdays, Easters and Christmases came and went. I didn't hear from Ann. I held out quiet hope that I might hear from her and other members of the family around the time of my fiftieth birthday. I'd planned a fabulous party, which gave cause for much excitement and distraction. It was just as well. A lot of exciting things were planned for 2015; I was in the throes of my university studies and had just secured a secondment into a new program area to work in Aboriginal wellbeing – a project I was passionate about. I'd banded together with a few beautiful kindred spirits to make some noise with instruments and microphones, in an unstoppable expression of our frustration with the political climate in Australia, which had just seen the Rudd-Gillard-Rudd-Abbot train wreck bestowed upon us. Encouraged by a fellow student, a film maker, to turn a script I'd written in class into a short film, I set things in place to enter it into a local arts festival, which meant I was I was going to make a movie bound by a deadline. All of those things happened – it was a year of incredible highs.

During winter, I took study leave from work to take a short course in Australian Indigenous Knowledge at Victoria University, under Professor Gary Foley. I heard he would blow my mind and challenge me. I was ready, and Foley did not disappoint. My mind and heart were awash with stories of injustice, lies, and history, which most of us will never fully realise. The five days of lectures were interrupted by a thrilling weekend where my band, Cranky Pants, made its live debut – raising money for a local group supporting people seeking asylum, who had been temporarily settled in our neighbourhood and surrounds. The fire in my belly had been fanned – I was burning up with passion and energy to channel into something that would make a difference to how the ruling class thinks and acts – affecting the lives of First Nations peoples in this country, and people fleeing persecution in their own countries to seek asylum in Australia. I could not tolerate the injustices served upon people by seemingly ignorant and cruel politicians and those who supported them.

Back at uni after the weekend, I was readier than ever. My

head was filled to the brim – constant drips of history quenched my thirst to learn and understand our lives. I wasn't there to make new friends or contacts necessarily, I was there to learn, read and get ready for my assignment. I enjoyed wandering around alone in the silent and relatively empty campus during the winter semester break.

As I crossed the quadrangle at lunchtime, out of nowhere I was suddenly consumed by an imagining of Ann. In my mind, I could see her home in Launceston, the place I'd visited only twice in reality, but countless times in my mind. I wondered if she was ok. I visualised her there in her house and wondered if she'd set up a bedroom downstairs, perhaps she might be unwell and have trouble getting up and down the stairs. I saw her in a white single bed in the lounge room with the open fireplace and red walls and red carpet she loved, and thought it seemed sensible. I was thinking about her big old house and all of the stuff that she would have in it and all of the books and things she collected over the years. I wondered what she would consider her most precious items. She was very proud of her pansy crockery collection she showed me on my first visit. She had an aunty called Pansy. I imagined what a huge job it would be for someone, most likely Madeline, to one day have to clear everything out of that house. It would be a huge job that would take months I thought. Anyway, it was an odd but very vivid stretch of imaginings I had, thinking about Ann like this. In reality, I actually had no idea if she was still in the house. There was a time when she'd contemplated selling and buying an inner-city warehouse with Madeline.

∞

A COUPLE OF NIGHTS later a text message arrived from my aunt Bronwyn – she wanted to come and see me. It was a shock to hear from her at all. I wondered if she had some bad news about Nana.

Bronwyn looked fine when she arrived at the doorstep. It had been over two years since I'd seen her. We hugged, but it was nothing like that first hug. As she sat at the kitchen table, I made coffee, shuffling between the table, the cupboard and the stove while she asked after the children and spoke about her son, my cousin, who was doing wonderful things overseas. I was disarmed by the chatter and forgot momentarily that she may have bad news about Nana. Finally, I sat down, both of us with mugs of coffee at hand.

'I have some bad news,' she said.

'Yes,' I said attentively and solemnly.

'Ann died on Tuesday.'

I felt a diesel truck drive right through me at high speed, leaving my empty outline in its wake.

'Ann?' I yelped. 'Ann died? She died? Ann?'

I began sobbing.

Oh no.

She died.

She's dead.

She's gone.

I'll never speak to her again.

I was in shock and completely gutted.

'How did she die?'

Thinking it must have come as a shock for everyone, I was surprised by the answer. 'She had cancer.'

And it slowly began to occur to me that people don't die of cancer overnight. She would have known for some time. Bronwyn continued speaking. Ann had requested I not be told about her illness. She was adamant and asked her sisters and her mother not to contact me. It felt like a powerful wind had swept my empty outline to the horizon. I was nothing. The truth was she had nothing more to say to me ever again. She made a firm decision, as she had when she chose to give me away the first time. She'd rejected me and any hope of reconciliation. She must have had no love left for me, she may have hated me. My heart, stomach, chest and throat were being continually stabbed as those thoughts rang loudly in my mind. She had nothing to say to me, ever again. I was stunned.

Bronwyn acknowledged my shock and suggested we move to the lounge room, where she covered me with a blanket as I sat staring into space. I was mostly silent, occasionally breaking it to gasp or sob.

'I feel like I've been pushed out into space, with no leads, no string, no net and nobody to hold me and look out for me,' I managed to say out loud.

'You have your family,' she responded.

How interesting she chose the word 'family'. I'd been pushed out and away by the woman who had done so before I was born, and after my birth. She'd pushed me away and try as she might, her pushing and forgetting and not telling anyone about me for thirty years did not negate my existence. She did her best to deny me. Until we reunited, it had worked. But then, she and her family, with a couple of exceptions, embraced me and drew me in and she expressed her gratitude and pride to me in many unconventional ways, usually without words, more with actions. I knew I was in her thoughts by the way she would remember the minutiae of my days, my friends' names, what I was working on, who I was working with. Her memory and attention to detail never failed to astound me. Her parcels of books and clothes and stuff for the house, for Andrew and the kids, and newspaper clippings and emails with links to articles she knew I'd find interesting. Her last act of denial wasn't just the whim of a dying woman. Her dying wish was to banish me. I couldn't hope for a last letter or something she may have left behind, something I could interpret as a message to dissolve the pain. There was nothing. I crumbled.

Bronwyn broke the silence across my lounge room by revealing that Ann's wishes were for no funeral or memorial. Nothing. She was donating her body for medical research, after which her ashes were to be given to her three children – which most definitely did not include me. She further requested her ashes be scattered at Rose Bay in Sydney, the place where she first met David fifty years ago – at a time and place when and where she carried me inside of her. I wonder if she considered me at all as she was constructing her final wishes. I wonder if she ever thought about me as she communicated her wishes about 'her children' or about 'the place where she met David'.

I can't be sure what it was like for her mother, siblings and other children to be told there would be no funeral. It may have been a relief for some of them. I dared to imagine Ann's funeral, where her favourite hymns would be sung, readings read and stories told that spoke of her greatest qualities, her achievements and even her failings. I imagined myself sitting in the last row, by the door in an unnamed chapel, ready to escape the glares of anyone who felt I had done wrong by asking Ann about my biological truth. Variations of the scenario played out in my mind in lieu of... nothing.

A practicing civil celebrant since 2008, I have created and officiated secular ceremonies such as weddings, funerals, naming ceremonies, hearth-warmings, and blessing-ways. I work with primary schools to create rites of passage programs with Grade 6 students transitioning to secondary school. Rituals and formalised celebrations of life's milestones have increasingly become important to me over the years, as my confidence and faith in formal religions has drastically waned. I've become more interested in cultural rituals and ceremony to connect families and communities to each other and their place. For every funeral or memorial I have worked on, whether for friends, family or strangers, I am privy to the raw emotional state of all involved. The preparation of a ceremony provides an important outlet for immediate kin, filled with complexities and emotions, surprises and tussles. I've walked away from funerals feeling like there had been a respectful ending. With some, I've left knowing more about that person than I did before, and others I've left feeling frustrated because elements aren't connected to the deceased person at all. Conducting a funeral or memorial well is an art – and just like art, it is subjective, there are bound to be critics. One of the many reasons cultures around the world ritualise death through ceremony is to show gratitude and respect, while coming to terms with grief and loss. There have been an infinite number of lines written and songs sung about death and dying, some questioning life and death and others lamenting grief and loss. One of the biggest questions I've often faced is this: Who is a funeral for? The departed, or the ones left behind?

As I sat on the lounge, covered with a blanket and in silence, I called Andrew and somehow muttered the few words I had. Within minutes – it felt like three, but must have been thirty – he was there. He sat with me in shock, holding me and not leaving my side for the rest of the day, or the next. I called my mum. She was shocked, but her feelings for Ann had diminished over the years, and I could not depend upon her unconditional empathy. She couldn't understand my agony, and I was reluctant to let her in for fear of causing her pain. Instead I relied on the rock beside me, Andrew, and together we tried to make sense of the sadness and betrayal.

It was a lot to take in. Apart from the grief, loss and pain, waves of anger and betrayal began to wash over me. I briefly became furious that she had shut me out of her ending, but more than that – she had taken her big secret, my paternity, to her death. She held all the cards, and she played them until the end. She showed me complete disregard by deciding her final word to me would be, her death. The ultimate 'fuck you.'

BLEEDING

Thursday, 18 June 2015

Today I found out that my birth mother Ann died two days ago on Tuesday 16 June at 3pm, in her home in Launceston, with her two (other) daughters by her side. It's over. It is the end. No further correspondence will be entered into. Not that it would have been anyway. We haven't been in contact since around March 2011, since I started asking questions about the identity of my biological father.

This is the third time Ann has died for me. Who's to say what her first death actually meant to me or what impacts it had. I was a baby when she let me go. I will never judge her wrongly for that decision, as I'm not convinced it was solely her own. A beautiful intelligent young woman, 21 years old, who had won a Commonwealth scholarship in chemistry I believe, to a university in Sydney, I don't even know which one. I've dreamed long and large about Ann's life in Sydney in those years, particularly around 1964, at the time I was conceived. I have always been on her side, always gone in to bat for Ann.

Her dad, Old Jim McGarry, I gather from the minimal accounts I've heard, was a force to be reckoned with. He's the one that made all of the arrangements for my adoption and he's the one who arranged for Ann to go on a cruise to Fiji to 'get over it'. He's also the one who chose to keep Ann's secret from everyone, presumably, and most regrettably, his wife, my Nana. I'd love to know more about the relationship Ann had with her dad, Old Jim. How did it happen that she chose him to confide in? How did it affect their relationship? Did they ever discuss the baby they let go? Did I ever enter their minds again?

I'm trying to make sense of the big story, of who I actually am and from whence did I come – or more like it, from whom did I come?

I must have been some novelty to my maternal family when they were told of my existence. They flocked from four states to meet me, with OPEN arms. I was so impressed by Ann, her hair, her manner, her language and her laughter. She was, however, odd in her outspoken and terse manner. It was not what I'd become used to at all. She could be bold and brash and bossy, in a cool way. She said it like it was and didn't fuss. She was a great hugger but also aloof with emotions. I thought that tremendous event, my birth, gave reason to many of her idiosyncrasies. It wasn't until much, much later that I started to realise it may have been her idiosyncratic behaviour, her emotional detachment, which enabled her to do what she did, and to behave the way she did – to turn on and then off, without warning – to encounter others on her own terms – to control.

I'm left to speculate about the woman who gave me life, whose genetic history I share. When I say genetic history, it sounds like a chemical equation in a Petri dish. It sounds so callous and cold. Like there could never be anything emotional or spiritual that could come from a genetic line. My heart is aching and breaking as I think how important that belonging is to me and how angry I am that it meant so little to her. The countless parcels she flooded us with; beautiful clothes, toys, books and items we loved and used, and also some we never needed or wanted. This went well beyond generosity. Was it some type of need to fulfil? I was always happy and grateful to receive her parcels, even though it overwhelmed me.

I heard somebody say on the TV last night that you don't realise the history or the revolution when you're inside of it, it's only in retrospect. Three years ago, when the devastating emotional nuclear bomb was dropped on my heart, I didn't realise it was the slow-burning death of my relationship with Ann. My need to know my paternity is something I will never apologise for, even though asking the question meant my relationship with Ann would never recover. I always held some hope that we would have contact again – I couldn't really believe that a woman from whom I descended, could refuse to contact me, or my children – her grandchildren – ever again. I always held a glimmer of hope deep inside of me. Yesterday that hope was snuffed. All hope of any further communication gone. She has taken it away from me. The whole family took it away from me when they agreed to not tell me Ann had cancer and was dying. I assume it was her dying wish. Her decision to let me go from her life was her decision. Again.

If I had known about her cancer, what would I have done? I would have thought long and hard about it, and like my letters and communications over time, I would have been respectful. If someone had told me my birth mother was dying, I expect I'd be told to not upset her. Is the truth upsetting? Can't it be liberating? I'll NEVER know why she couldn't tell me anything about my paternity, apart from the fact the guy used a condom, and he was Italian – 'for what it's worth.'

Not only will I never know that important part of my story, a truth that has been knowingly withheld, I never got the chance to tell her I love her and that I was so happy to have had the chance to meet her and to be included, for a time, in her family and her story. For a long time, I actually did feel that she loved me and that she was proud of me and that she saw some of herself in me. I was proud she was my birth mother and so fulfilled to see and feel a family connection like I'd never experienced.

Every time a baby is born and from then throughout their lives as children, to teenagers into adulthood, people are always being referenced to their family; their looks, behaviours, and choices. 'Oh, he's so much like...' 'Oh, she's the image of...' It is everywhere and it is something that I have been acutely aware of my whole life, because it NEVER applied to me. I wanted my own family history, my own family tree and my own family truth. I got tired a long time ago from adopting another family's truth. Their stories are not my stories. I love my family, but their stories are not true for me.

–

It's now Monday, 22 June 2015 and I've had a few days to process what has happened. I can't even say that I understand what has happened, apart from the fact that someone has died. It's more than a death to me. It's betrayal, rejection, abandonment, deception and manipulation. Those words cut deep and I feel a huge pain in my chest. I don't want to be angry, but now and then I'm overwhelmed with anger, then it passes, for something else. Deep, deep sadness. She must have hated me so much to push me away and to be so cruel.

I respect and admire cultures who revere their elders and who hold mothers up for adoration yet at the same time I'm thankful that I can actually confront the awful truth that not all mothers and elders are worthy of our respect. There are cruel people, and some become cruel with age. Ann must have really hated me and what I'll never know is, before she hated me, what did she think of me? I will never know. It seemed at that initial stage of contact she was more than happy that I'd found her. I was this big secret, and she was good at perpetuating secrecy. It seems she has died with a bunch of secrets. It truly pains me to say something negative about my dead mother. It is actually awful. I hate that. That is how I feel. She was selfish and cruel to me. You hear all the time how good things happen to good people – well that's absolute bullshit. That's just some dogma to keep us all toeing the line. Be good so that good things will happen to you. It's a reduction of the karmic philosophy which can provide temporary relief from a festering sore, but true infections need something stronger.

I'm from a culture that expects us to revere and respect our elders, our mothers and fathers and grandparents. This is why I have trouble saying things like 'she was a selfish and cruel woman'. I want my kids and their kids to respect me and love me because I respect and love them. That said, I've had to come to terms with the fact that awful people (with some exceptions) can have redeeming qualities, what

I'll call 'goodness' in them. My realisation on the weekend, in a bath, where all great thoughts happen – and I don't have nearly enough baths – was that humanity at large would benefit so much if we all acknowledged the dark history of those we were borne from, and just took forward their goodness. If each generation took only the goodness from their forebears, wouldn't humanity and our planet thrive?

Now I'm waiting... waiting for the ticking time bomb to explode. I'm unsure in the silence of my home; I can hear the wind howling outside, the occasional siren of distress coming into the fore and fading past, inside I hear the kitchen clock ticking, alternating with the dripping kitchen tap. Together they sound like time is accelerating but at the same time, time seems to be dragging. The tick, tap, tick, tap – I'm so conscious that there is something else to come. Maybe that something is a big, fat SILENCE, from everyone. So Ann's dying wish was for nobody to tell me she was dying of cancer, since last July – twelve months. What were her instructions after she died? Is there an embargo on how long it will be before anyone can speak with me? What if there was nothing said and while my family is free from the spell of the dying wish, they still say nothing? What am I responsible for? Who is going to be the first to break? So far there has been the words of my cousin Emma, which resounded so large through my being that they broke me down. She has admitted the cruelty and the deception and apologised for her part. Seeing it in print confirmed my worst thoughts. I knew all of those things before I read her message, but seeing it written down, I was absolutely gutted. Now, a couple of days later, I realise she was put in an awful position. I'm blown away by the unwritten law of this family. What were the consequences for anyone breaking the rules? What is the payoff for doing as you're told?

I've never been in the position to keep the confidence of a dying person. It might be the cause of a huge ethical dilemma. If I had known Ann was dying, what would I have done? I could have prepared myself, even though her death from me became a reality three years ago. I may have wanted to write to her, I don't know. I would have probably sent her something. Probably a photo of me, her daughter, with my family, to show her that despite her life of secrets and choices to abandon and deceive and exclude us, the four of us are solid. We are truly solid. Maybe that would have given her some peace, closure. I will never know.

Getting back to this ticking time bomb, there's a part of me setting up the other part of me for another major disappointment. There's a part of me that is hoping for a message from beyond her grave. Maybe she left something for me, some words, thoughts or a final gesture. Of course I'm thinking it would be heartfelt and confessional in nature and would finally indicate her care, if not love for me. However, the flipside of that little daydream is dread. I'm dreading that she has left something for me and that it would be another screw into my heart, to hurt me and to reject me, all over again. So here I am, waiting for something which could be great or devastating, or waiting for nothing, which would be devastating. And that's just from Ann.

I'm also waiting for something, or nothing, from members of the family. In order to protect myself, I need to set my expectations low.

It's hard for me, because, as my family, as the people from where I came, I can't believe that without the shackles of a dying wish, these people will just leave me out there. Hanging, mid-air, without a net. Nestling under a big blanket on the lounge, I told Bronwyn that's how I felt. I felt like she pushed my chest with a really long pole, pushing me further into an abyss; 'You have your family to support you,' she said. Once upon a time, she was my family. They were all my family. The novelty has worn off and I'm some kind of thorn in their side. I replied in a whisper, 'I'm not a bad person, I'm not a bad person at all.' She said nothing. She did not respond. She just let me hang out there. So, she and they must really think I am a bad person! I can't believe it! Because I wanted to know my paternity? Is that what she told them? What did she say? Did they all just nod their heads and agree? Did anyone try to talk to her at all? Did she ever get any professional counsel?

—

A weird thing is...

I recalled the story of the vision I had of Ann earlier in the week when I was walking across the quadrangle at uni, and described what I'd seen to Bronwyn just after she told me Ann had died. She seemed interested but was quite adamant that Ann was still in her bedroom upstairs, as she had been some time ago when Bron visited her for what was to be her last time. She said it was very nice as Ann had access to her bathroom and a lovely view out of her window, onto the river and rooftops and trees. 'Oh,' I responded, 'how lovely for her,' or some such. While it's an innate response to be kind and respectful of elderly and sick parents, some of what Bronwyn was telling me was making me angry. A little later she recalled that in fact the palliative care people had come to Ann's place about a week earlier with a new bed and set Ann up in the lounge room downstairs, just as I had imagined/envisioned. I've told a few people that story since, and some say it was very special and that Ann was probably thinking about me at the same time. I'd like to think that was the case but it's more likely that my subconscious just took me there for a one-way visit. I don't think it was reciprocated, because I now feel like she didn't give a shit about me at best, and hated me at worst.

After Bronwyn broke the news to me, she went on with some of the details... Madeline and Jacinta were holding her hands when she died.

'Madeline has been so wonderful, nursing and caring for Ann. She'd go out every day to do errands and get medication and have the phone with her at all times. She's been amazing.'

All the while I wanted to scream...

'Why the fuck didn't anyone tell me she was dying?'

'You all kept it from me!'

'What do you think of me?'

'Do you think I have no rights?'

'How could everyone have lied to me, kept it from me, deceived and manipulated me?'

'Whatever did I do wrong?'

'I have a right to ask the question that ALL adopted children ask... "Who is my father?"'

—

The obituary was placed in the Sydney Morning Herald by Ann's sister Prudence:

> **Elizabeth Ann.**
> 17.1.1944 – 16.6.2015
> Loving wife of David (dec). Loved mother of Jacinta, Madeline and Michael. Ann is survived by her children, her mother Enid and her siblings.
>   At her request Ann has donated her body for medical research.
>   Upon their return her ashes will be scattered by her children at the water front in Double Bay NSW where she met David.

Another bolt to my heart. Without mention. The scattering will take place where not only did Ann meet David, but where she lived while pregnant with me, 51 years ago.

Once again, my existence was denied and I struggled to believe I was so obviously written out of public records. I contemplated a reply in the online guest book, tossing and turning my options and decisions like flipping pancakes. After several weeks I decided to add a comment.

As I opened the tab that took me to the website to find the guest book for death notices, I discovered the period of one month paid for by the family had expired, yesterday.

My message would have read:

> **To Ann** - the woman who gave birth to me 51 years ago. I will be forever grateful we were united after thirty years, that you witnessed great love at my wedding to Andrew, and that you knew wonder in the lives of your only grandchildren, Angus and Brigit. We will be forever connected.
> Your daughter, Karen

I would have written myself and my children into Ann's family history, to be recognised by those living today, and for future generations to find us. In the writing of my story, I claim my place – and that of my children and their children – in the McGarry and Harris family histories.

A short time after receiving the shocking news, on a clear and cold Melbourne winter's night I sat in my backyard with some close friends around a fire, and spoke some difficult truths. I needed to retell what had happened, in a way so that I could believe it, so I could grapple with my pain, that I might gain clarity and reason as to why things happened the way they did. It wasn't a ceremony of any kind, just a fire with friends and mulled wine. In the preparation, the act of inviting others, tidying the house, writing the shopping list for ingredients – I was too fragile to venture out into the world – words began to surface about what I wanted to say about Ann. This is what I said:

From what I knew about Ann she was lively, fun, generous, quirky, intelligent, gregarious and beautiful. Despite some of my more recent misgivings she was, in her own way, wise. She had a peculiar way with people – she could be abrupt, dismissive, terse, very determined and fiercely independent. She lived with a huge secret for thirty years – that she became pregnant before she was married, to a man who was not her boyfriend. After giving birth she gave her baby away.

Ann, I get the pain of making as huge a mistake as getting pregnant and relinquishing a baby, although you never spoke to me of any of that. I'm still unsure how sad you were about giving me away. I wouldn't be surprised that, in your pragmatic way, you just took care of business and locked that part of your life, the bit about me and my conception and all of that time, in a box, locked it up, bound it with chains and locked them up and threw away the keys. Perhaps you couldn't open the box even if you wanted to because the keys were long gone.

Now you are dead and I can only speculate and continue to wonder about you. There were dinners and lunches and picnics and cheese and wine and some birthdays and even carols by candlelight. There were afternoon teas and shopping and bus trips and phone calls and emails and parcels and Christmas gifts and birthday presents. I thought we had as much as a connection as you would have with anyone.

And so, as your daughter, your firstborn child, if genetics and biological heritage mean anything at all, I aim to take the best parts of your character and carry them forward. I aim to be aware of any of your traits that caused me so much pain as they emerge in me. I believe that's the best any of us can do, to take the best from the people who have gone before us and learn from their actions that caused harm. We cannot change the past, but we have a hand in the present and a foot in the future.

In a jumbled, inebriated state that's what I attempted to say around the fire that night, clutching my glass of warm mulled wine as it chilled in the dark and dank air. I held onto those warm sentiments, trying to save them before they chilled, as I sipped the wine while it remained warm.

THE GLASS BOWL – PART 2

Fourteen years after our wedding day, fourteen years since I'd met Ann and she'd gifted us the rose-coloured glass bowl, it came crashing and smashing to the lounge room floor, a shocking casualty of the frolics of our new kittens. I struggled with the loss of such an important piece, her first precious gift. I considered its symbolism, what it might portend, and failed to see how anything could shatter the bond we'd formed since we'd met.

I was wrong.

As I swept up the petals in the dust off the floor, among the rose-coloured glass shards, I noticed they'd lost their colour and scent, they were dry and brittle and the words they contained upon their first shower over me were long gone.

Reflecting on that photo today, I'm struck by the lost, cold and withered sentiments of that time. The words had changed into a source of pain, pain that was showered upon me by her hand.

    Shock   Grief   Loss

    Betrayal   Mistrust

Misunderstood   Fractured   Suspended

    Power   Silence

I cannot escape her beauty and the love she had for me at certain times. I was in her mind if no longer in her heart.

PASSING ON, DOWN, THROUGH

Almost two months after Ann's death, the world looked the same but felt different. My axis had taken a hit. On my way to the funeral of my friend's father, a call came from my aunt. I didn't pick it up, as I was about to walk into a church. Afterwards I was in Fitzroy on my way to have lunch with a friend, before having my hair cut at a place which had an eight-week waiting list. I returned the call and this time my earlier hunch was right. Bronwyn called me to say that Nana had died that morning. She had found Ann's death very difficult to deal with, and being in frail health in her ninety-sixth year, she'd taken her last breath. I was utterly grateful I had that chance to sit with Nana four months prior. I felt she died with us knowing and understanding each other. I felt her love and did my best to show her mine. The rest of my day went in slow motion. Bron generously told me Nana would've loved to have known I was treating myself to a special day at the hairdresser. It was hard to be mindful and present for my appointment, as my mind became cluttered with thoughts for Nana, the time we were afforded and the missing years. On a whim, I encouraged Andrew to leave work early and join me for a toast to Nana on the rooftop of a Fitzroy bar, Naked for

Satan. Bron had made it very clear that there would be a private funeral for Nana, an obvious code for 'you're not invited'. My presence in the family remained uncomfortable. I looked over the Fitzroy rooftops to find the Dandenong Ranges on the horizon, raised my glass of bubbles in her name, to show my deep gratitude and respect for a most remarkable woman. My Nana. The doors on two lives that loomed large in my life had closed in a short space of time. To think or hope of finding my biological truth overwhelmed me. The key to that treasure box had been burned with its keeper. Was there any other way? The time I'd spent with Nana hearing more about her life had fuelled the smouldering embers I'd been distracted from – the family history I'd wanted to pursue under the guidance of my older aunt, Prudence. Since those ties had been severed, I'd let it slide. Then, out of the blue, I was made an incredible offer.

HISTORIES AND TRUTHS

The wonderful Teddie is the mother of a friend, and an historian. She'd been recently working on an all-consuming project and was keen for a distraction. Knowing a little of my story, she offered to undertake some family research for me. This news, and her passion and expertise, was a soul saver. She sent many updates and riveting revelations to my inbox each week. This was what I needed. A huge slice of my maternal history, which nobody else could tell me, was unfolding before my eyes at a rapid pace. Finally, I was finding a connection with my ancestors, having a glimpse into their lives, relationships and the places they called home, in New South Wales, Tasmania and before that, in England and Ireland.

These stories started to work in a strange parallel to the family history of my adoptive family. The place where Nana's family settled in the Hunter Valley was very close to the place of Mum's forebears. My aunts and uncles were buried in Anglican church graveyards in the Hunter Valley, as were those of Mum. Thinking of a connection to place and finding ancestral homelands, I started to feel more connected to a place that had been part of my adoptive folklore – realising the commonalities across two families of familiar places and people, the landscape, the stories and the names. My quivering emotional core started to settle with this newfound knowledge, as I started to fit the pieces together. For a long while I holidayed in the past, and took great comfort in learning these family truths from what could be gathered from official documents – including some salacious media reports.

As had been the case for more than twenty years, my thoughts returned to my Italian heritage and the identity of my father. I could easily find distractions but the big question would always return. Who was my father? As I continued to tell my story to friends and confidantes, an awful and ugly question appeared. I strongly believe that Ann knew the identity of Condom Man, and if her unplanned pregnancy was the result of a spontaneous fling up a back lane with a stranger, she had every chance to say so – as I mentioned to her many times, without judgement. Her shocked reaction to the truth about the DNA test with Silvio was telling, as she refused to divulge any further information. Perhaps she was ashamed or embarrassed, which I understand, and I would have been so happy to work through that with her. I didn't, however, accept that as a fitting reason to withhold vital information about me, from me. Perhaps she was protecting someone. Perhaps she was raped, and it was important to her that she never revisit that memory again. Perhaps, perhaps, perhaps.

It was interesting she chose her father as the only one to tell about her pregnancy. It's unclear exactly the nature of their relationship – she was his firstborn, who chose to follow in his footsteps to become a pharmacist. An ugly question arose – posed by people close to me, as they thought long and hard about the facts I had presented. It wasn't until one of them asked me directly, out loud, face-to-face, that I was jolted to a halt. 'Could Old Jim be your father?' The possibility I could have been born as a result of an incestuous relationship started to chew at me from the inside out. Many scenarios had crossed my mind, and this one was too awful to bear. I convinced myself that if this was indeed the truth, I would make it my business to make the most of the situation – trying very hard to rise above that outcome, considering all the children who had been born out of similar 'relationships'. Too horrid to bear, alright. I'd been an avid and passionate supporter of victims of childhood sexual abuse, especially that of fathers against their children, so yes – it would be the ugliest, most horrible pill to swallow. I would do it to show my children that we were ok, and that others in the same boat are ok, and that they should not be judged harshly as a result of the actions of others.

Many friends suggested I take a commercial DNA test to explore my ancestry, but I resisted. I didn't know what it would prove. It's not like I'd get my big question answered… Da-da… Your father is—!

'Have you had one of those DNA tests?' They'd ask.

'My sister did it and now we know (what we already knew) that we are as Irish as whiskey!'

And then there's the ads! My cynicism kicks in. It's a ploy, it's a business, it's a giant data bank, a bank of genetic material. The more customers, the more effective they'll be and the more customers they'll attract, from all over the world, in their quest for cultural identity.

I also felt uneasy about a giant bank of DNA results being stored in some warehouse or data-farm in the United States. To me, these tests served the purpose of a corporation over and above that of people searching for answers. I dilly-dallied over this for more than a year until I came to my senses and just did it. My main motivation was to eliminate Old Jim as my father. I concluded that if the test results revealed I had NO Italian heritage, then I would be faced with a much stronger possibility that indeed it could be Old Jim. If the results showed I had Italian heritage, then this would discount the possibility. Sure, my DNA would be on file in the US for millennia; it could be used in a cyborg attack against western democracy or captured during an alien invasion. Maybe I'd be cloned. As a friend pointed out, I've disclosed enough personal information on social media and by signing petitions that my identity was ripe for thieving years ago. I may have had a bit to lose, but I had one big answer to gain.

I really need to get a grip and not lose sight of my holy grail. That is… my cultural identity. Where does it sit? Where do I fit? And so, I did. I paid for a kit, received a code, spat into a vial, posted it off and awaited the results. Simple.

I wanted the test results to confirm my Italian heritage. However, should there be NO Italian heritage found then my suspicions would be going to one of the deepest, darkest corners that I had ever considered. My search so far had revealed many things and so much remains hidden. Who was Condom Man?

Could the man whom Ann couldn't speak about anymore be someone who was a threat to her? Could he be someone close to her that would bring shame? Could he be someone who caused so much unbearable pain that he had been locked up in a box by thousands of links on a hundred chains, fastened by a dozen locks? Could it be? Could it be that the bossy older man, who made all of the arrangements for my adoption, was my father as well as my grandfather? Could it be that I am a product of an incestuous relationship between my birth mother and her father? It could explain some things. It might give reason for her pain, and bring about more pain and shame than I've ever known. If this is the truth, then I must find a way to live with it, to reconcile and to make a mark with it. I would have to declare it – the whole rotten, vile truth. This is what I must eliminate or validate.

The results came in and I was quick to jump to the bottom line. The relief! I was elated with my 'score' of fifty percent combined Italian and Iberian heritage; the rest was English/Irish. The weight off my heart was immense. It was one giant step taken to get closer to my truth.

A GRAND IMAGINING

During the minutes and hours I allowed my mind to drift, to wander and imagine, just like I had when I was a little girl, I became immersed in a recurring scenario. I found my fantastical thinking endlessly amusing, and the longer it brewed within and poured without to my trusted people, the more cinematic it became.

∞

TONIGHT IS THE REOPENING of the Mandalay and the most important reunion of my life. The old place will soon be full of strangers who, as a collective, have an important role to play. Surrounded by the dull roar of afternoon traffic, I focus on the doorway surrounded by flashing lights. From my first step into the foyer I am cocooned in red and gold, the spongy carpet and the velveteen embossed swirls on the walls reflect in the gilded framed mirrors. It is set-up time. Small round tables are draped to the floor and set with lamps. Finishing touches are being made to a shimmering silver and gold backdrop and the red velvet curtain front of stage, and a couple of techs adjust microphones and tidy leads. The slow spin of the mirror ball fills the empty room, which is both haunting and exhilarating. Two hours until showtime.

The ding on my phone alerts me to a text. It's the lab. They've arrived and are awaiting further instructions.

'I'll meet you in the side lane in two minutes.'

My covert and ambitious operation is underway. The square white van barely manages to squeeze down the lane. It's bigger than I'd expected. I approach with trepidation as the side door slides open to reveal two men and two women wearing white coats and what look like shower caps. This is the business. A business I don't fully understand, which is why I require experts. Man 1 goes over the instructions and hands me twelve clear plastic tubes, a handful of stickers and a marker pen.

'It is important you write a name or other means of identification on the sticker and place it onto the tube.'

I take them from him, looking carefully and my mind buzzes with a cacophony of sounds, it's dizzying. Do not lose it now, I tell myself through clenched teeth. Stay calm and in control. This is coming together.

'Yes, right, u-huh, ok.' As I'm about to ask, he interrupts my thoughts.

'These are the swabs. You need to keep them sealed until such time as the samples are taken. When you're ready, remove the wrapping and take the sample.'

I concentrate hard on the instructions.

'You've done this before, right?' he continues.

'Yes. OK. And then I'll bring them to you, and you do what you do, and you'll have the results for me how soon?'

'We'll know if there's a match within 40 minutes.'

This step is crucial to my plan. Tonight we will be eliminating suspects and I will know which member of the band is my father.

There is still a bit to organise. I have to meet with the MC and get dressed to impress. Red and gold have always looked fabulous on me, but I hadn't factored in just how well I was going to fit in with the venue. From the front door to the stage to the... makeshift lab parked in the lane. The owners of the new Mandalay are friends of friends from the old days. They are very accommodating and don't ask too many questions which is perfect – given I have no answers, only big concepts. They allocate me a small and comfortable dressing room fitted with an ensuite and multiple mirrors in a range of sizes – most importantly the full-length mirror. The lighting is superb. The next best thing about my dressing room is that it's stage left, adjacent to the external doorway into the lane, and on the other side of the stage to the large dressing room that is being used by the band.

Another ding. Another text. The MC is running late. I call him back, tell him what I need him to do and how it fits into the night's proceedings. I leave him written instructions with the night manager.

It is a momentous occasion for the Mandalay and those who know her. In Sydney throughout the sixties, the Mandalay had been a popular supper club among the emerging Italian community and Australians who appreciated the music, fashion, character and effervescent vivant. The house band played a mix of classic dancehall tunes from the old country and popular music by the jazz and lounge crooners of the times.

Some of the Australian clientele included a regular group of young women who were taken by the exotic accents and well-heeled manners and looks of the Italian men, particularly the boys in the band.

I hear the arrival of the band from my dressing room. Loud greetings and Italian chatter. My heart races as I slip into my fabulous vintage cocktail frock. A knock on the door startles me out of my daydream. It's the manager with a bottle of champagne in an ice bucket and a couple of glasses. I pour a glass of golden bubbles and go through a mental checklist of exactly what I have to do. Looking over the plastic tubes and wrapped swabs, the stickers and the pen it's obvious some careful choreography is needed. The bubbles jolly intoxication through every vein in my body, my arms, my groin, my legs and toes. My cheeks blush and after I finish my glass I swish Revlon Red across my lips, blot, empty the ice from the bucket and place the swabs inside. A final check in the mirror, a big smile and an affirming exclamation, 'Fabulous!' I walk out the door.

Doors to the public are opening in twenty minutes and a thick, sticky aroma of expectation fills every corner of the room. The spirits are stirring and my heart is skipping. I reserve a table in the front row, next to the dance floor, where I place my ice bucket and then find my way to side of stage where the MC prepares his notes. He looks up as I sashay toward him. We share a brief introduction and check the schedule. I can tell I impress him and that he will do anything I ask. Brushing past him with an outrageous air of confidence I make my way backstage to the band's dressing room. Silvio greets me with a warm hug and kiss to both of my blushing cheeks. He is thrilled to see me. The men stop their chatter, stop what they are doing and look at me. It's as if they've seen a ghost. Silvio introduces me.

'You remember Ann? Ann McGarry? This is her daughter, Karen!'

The silence breaks with resounding Italian chatter. Many hold their looks in my direction and speak among themselves. Gionni comes to greet me and Frank crosses the room toward me with a leering smile. 'You are as beautiful as your mother' he says as he takes my hand in both of his.

I greet them all as a group, smile and tell them how exciting it is to be here.

'I've been told that my mother enjoyed many wonderful nights here. I'm really looking forward to hearing your music and I've arranged a special surprise this evening, so I will see you shortly. Good luck!'

Their chatter increases as I leave them to prepare to take the stage. As I return to my seat, the doors open and the room rapidly fills with the excited sounds of the audience – mostly family and friends of the Mandalay, old and new. I take my seat, the house lights dim and the MC takes the stage.

'Ladies and gentlemen, *bongiorno*, good evening and welcome to THE MANDALAY! It's been a long time between drinks and...'

The volume of his voice recedes in my mind, overtaken by my deafening internal chatter.

This is it!

I can't believe it!
What am I doing?
How did I manage this?
What will happen?
What do they think of me?
What will they think of me?
Can I pull this off?
I just want to know the truth!
What if I never find out the truth?
I have a right to know.
This is absurd!
This is the only way.

The band plays, and the people dance. My internal organs pound yet I feel paralysed. I am unable to dance. I am focused on what I am about to do.

The MC takes to the stage, back-announces the last set and introduces the members of the band. One by one, he announces their names and one by one each musician gestures to the audience, to their fellow musicians, smiling and waving, clearly thrilled to be performing onstage after so many years. I eye off each man carefully as I search for any clue of their former association with Ann. The internal chatter echoes loudly:

What did you think of Ann?
Were you her friend?
Were you ever her lover?
Were you a player?
What do you know?

Do you remember?

Are you covering something up?

Could it be you?

Momentarily distracted by my own internal chatter, I almost miss my cue. I snap back into the moment at the sound of my name through the speakers.

'....special friend of the Mandalay, Ann's daughter Karen!'

The spotlight blinds me as I pick up the ice bucket, and a sloppy half drum roll accompanies my ascension to the stage. Reminiscent of a 1960s television game show, I take part in a Q&A with the MC, with enforced smiles, oversized gestures and our best ever radio voices. In a duo, like Bob and Dolly Dyer, or Tony Barber and Barbie Rogers, the MC and the hostess/barrel girl begin their onstage repartee.

MC: Welcome to the Mandalay, Karen!

Me: Why thank you very much, Bradley, it is an absolute pleasure to be here. May I also say, you are doing a sterling job this evening.

MC: Oh Karen, thank you very much! Now I understand you have a special connection with the Mandalay. Can you tell us something about that?

Me: As a matter of fact, I can Bradley. Back in 1963 and 1964 my mother used to do quite a bit of socialising at the Mandalay with her friends. I understand she was quite taken with the good-looking, fun-loving and talented Italians who played in the band here.

A 'boom-tish' sound of the drums is accompanied by a short and embarrassed giggle from some of the band members.

MC: That's very interesting, Karen, because the band we have playing for us tonight, is the very same band that used to play at the Mandalay back in 1963 and 1964!

Me: Ah yes, Bradley, I believe so.

MC: So Karen, what brings you to the stage tonight, and what is in that ice bucket in you're holding. It doesn't look like champagne to me!

Me: Ha! Ha! Bradley. It is a very exciting night for me and it will be a VERY exciting evening for one of the men on the stage. You see I'm on a bit of a treasure hunt and I need all of the members of the band to play along with me, to help me find my treasure.

MC: A treasure hunt, Karen?

Me: Yes, Bradley, a treasure hunt.

MC: Can you tell us what the treasure is you're looking for?

Me: Bradley, I can. I am looking for my biological father.

A sharp and sudden 'boom-tish' sounds from the drums.
 An audible gasp from the audience

MC: Your father?

 Me (Smiling broadly): Yes Bradley, that's right, my father.

MC: Well how are you going to find this man?

Me: Well that's why I need this! (I hold the ice bucket in the air)

MC: (Looking into the ice bucket) That looks like cotton buds and test-tubes!

Me: You're getting very warm, Bradley. What we have here are SWABS! (Smiling broadly). Now what I'm about to do is obtain a friendly saliva swab from each of the darling men on the stage. With your help, Bradley, I will label these plastic tubes with the name of the person who belongs to the sample. And, with the help of everyone in the audience, as my witnesses, we will collect DNA and have it tested.

MC: Now that's some treasure hunt, Karen!

Me: But wait Bradley, there's more!

MC: More?

Me: That's right, there's more! Not only are we collecting the samples from these darling men tonight, but by the end of the show, I will be announcing the results!

Gasping sounds and chatter from the audience.

MC: Oh Karen, this really is adding more excitement to a very exciting evening of entertainment.

Me: Well Bradley, I could not let a chance like this slip by. To have all of these men in the one place at the one time, together again after so many years, it really is the PERFECT occasion to conclude my treasure hunt, once and for all.

MC: Well let's get started!

One by one, I approach each of the musicians, I hand him the swab and explain how to use it. In some instances, I need to assist, ensuring saliva content and consistency. Bradley announces the names of each sampler, writes the name on the sticker and places it on the plastic tube. With the finesse of a magician and her assistant, each swab is placed in a labelled plastic tube, witnessed and confirmed by the audience. We work through the band as a rhythmic groove is provided in turn by drums, bass, keyboards, piano accordion and guitar. The sample collection ends with a mighty 'boom-tish!'

MC: Well Karen, it looks like the samples have been collected. What next?

Me: (Smiling broadly)Thank you, Bradley, and a special, huge and heartfelt thanks to you gentlemen for taking part in my treasure hunt. Please, ladies and gentlemen, join me in a round of applause.

Clapping from the audience.

Me: What next? I'd like to call upon the operator of Mobile Genetics who has a team onsite, and who will undertake the relevant testing to ensure an accurate, verified and certified result within the hour.

Man 1 in white coat arrives onstage to accept the ice bucket of labelled samples.

MC: In all of my years as MC, this would have to be a first. This is the most exciting treasure hunt I've ever seen! Thank you to Mobile Genetics and most of all, thank you Karen! You have mastered quite a spectacle here this evening at the Mandalay. Ladies and gentlemen, let's hear it for our superb band tonight and show your appreciation in a huge round of applause. Please enjoy the rest of their set which will include a finale to top all finales, with a VERY important announcement!

As the band plays with a mix of bewilderment and bemusement, the men and women in the white van in the lane get down to business. I retreat to my dressing room to take stock, and most importantly, to replenish my glass of champagne and my Revlon Red. Minutes remain before I'll have my answer. The band is playing with an increased tempo. People are dancing and swinging and laughing and drinking. The Mandalay looks, sounds and feels like it could have fifty-one years ago. I take my place at my table and soak up every ounce of the atmosphere. I'm on the verge of something big. I allow myself to be carried away by the tunes and the people. Knowing that I can't stop what's been started, I surrender to the process.

I feel a tap on my shoulder. It is Man 1. It's difficult to hear his serious tone as he hands me a sealed envelope with the answer to my treasure hunt contained within.

The band's final song comes to an end and MC Bradley jumps onto the stage without missing a beat.

MC: Thank you, thank you, thank you! Ladies and gentlemen, members of the band, as this wonderful evening draws to an end, we have one very important announcement to make. For that, I'd like to call upon Karen to make her way to the stage.

To the sounds of the same rhythmic groove played by the band during the sample collection, I take my time walking to the stage, realising that this is the final moment of not knowing, of the feeling I've fought hard to overcome for many years. I approach the microphone, with the sealed envelope tightly clasped in my hand. Evoking the spirits of barrel girls around the world who have gone before me, I take a deep breath, give the biggest smile imaginable and announce...

'The Winner Is...'

DEAR DAD

The beauty of getting older is that we have so many memories to draw upon and by thinking back and recalling the big events, lots of random small things are remembered. I've often marvelled at the little things, and often find myself speaking in full voice to others or in a whisper to myself the phrase 'It's the little things' several times. It's the little things that can loom largest in our minds and our hearts, and that we can take great comfort in recalling. Memories of you are prompted by the expected and unexpected.

My years as a child at the time seemed endless and, while I was in a hurry to grow up, I did love being a child. I loved the safety and security that surrounded me in my loving home. One of my earliest memories was waving you goodbye at the front door in Vides Street as you left for work in the mornings. Some mornings would be extra exciting as a short time after the wave-off at the front door I'd stand on the back doorstep with a tea towel in my hand, waiting for the Sydney Flyer to zoom along the railway tracks in perfect sight. I furiously waved the tea towel and tried to catch a glimpse of you waving your rolled-up newspaper in the window of the train, just for me. For those seconds, I really felt you were waving just to me and did I feel special! I also felt a little sad to think you were travelling a long time on a train to the big city and hoped it wouldn't be long before you came home. Sometimes you stayed more than one day. Once I remember you brought me home a present. It certainly wasn't expected, and how surprised I was to receive a packet of textas – you made me feel pretty darn special.

Weekends were usually spent watching or listening to you do the jobs that needed doing around the house and yard, and I know your favourite job wasn't a job at all – it was the hours you loved to spend in the garden. Tending and nurturing fruit or flower-bearing plants, and the shrubs too, always provided you with enjoyment. But what you probably don't know is that it provided all of us with pride and enjoyment. We were glad you were content, challenged, interested and peaceful. This is still true to this day. Funnily enough, you didn't combine your love and talent for gardening with your other great talent, whistling. I guess you liked to keep your indoor and outdoor specialties separate.

To me, you have always been an action man. You always showed your love and care for me by doing. Ever since I can remember, all through my childhood and into adulthood, you have done things. You used to polish my school shoes, drive me to the bus or the train, you would make my lunch, often the night before, and set the bench for breakfast. You didn't do all of those things just because you loved me, of course. You were being time efficient, but I felt the love in my shiny shoes and my foil-wrapped lunch. I'll never forget the morning I heard your voice booming up the aisle of the 362, telling everyone, rather loudly, your daughter had forgotten her lunch, after you chased my school bus in your car. Despite the embarrassment, I knew you did it because you loved me and you looked after me. When I tell my children this story, I tell it with pure love, even as all of my senses relive every long second of that one minute. So many memories of you, Dad, and the ones I long for are the ones when as a little girl I felt the safest, when I was in your arms at the beach. You held me over every wave, up, over and down. I grabbed hold of you tight around your neck and you never let me down. There is so much more to you, the man who is my dad. From what I know you have been diligent, honest, capable, loving and caring. There are likely to be lots of other things I don't know about you, but this is about my memories of you. There are too many memories for this page, but never enough for my mind and my heart.

DEAR MUM

It's funny what can trigger a memory. Smells, sights and the sounds of words strung together by a stranger on the radio, or by a child. Sometimes a song or the sound of a familiar voice that has been etched into my soul. The voice I cannot remember not knowing. The sound of the voice of my mum.

We had many conversations over the years. After-school chats as I sat on the cane lounge eating your date loaf and drinking orange juice from those tall, mottled, smoked glasses. It was usually me doing all of the talking, and you always listening, offering kind interjections, asking questions and being interested. We laughed and we cried. Talking came quite naturally to both of us, especially in the car, on short trips where we covered thousands of topics. During longer trips I often fell asleep, and I was sorry to have left you alone in the car, driving miles and kilometres, going through gallons and litres of petrol.

Of course, we've had many talks over the phone, maybe more than we've had in person, as we've lived apart in different cities for a long time now. While I can't pretend to remember everything we've ever talked about, I certainly remember the essence. The essence of the love between us, sometimes spoken about, sometimes not. Certainly it's true that we haven't agreed on everything, but I'm quite ok with that. The essence we've shared has endured.

Your reassuring voice, your kind words when I've needed them most, the love and concern you have always expressed for my family, have meant the world to me. When I was in hospital after the births of my babies, your voice was the one I wanted to hear. You didn't seem far away at all, you were right there, in my ear, in my mind and in my heart.

Time has stretched longer between the sounds of your voice during different stages in my life. When you moved to Melbourne and I remained in Newcastle, without a home phone and long before mobiles, I think it was about a month that went by without us speaking. I remember Neil coming around to my place in King Street, firmly prompting me to give you a call. You see, I felt that you were never far away from me, you were always there. When Andrew and I travelled the world for six amazing months, there was no email. Yes, postcards – but I'm not sure I sent many of those. I think there were two phone calls home to you from public phones, the clunky hungry ones that gobbled down the coins. You did feel a little more distant from me then, but I never doubted that, like a boomerang, I'd return, if not a little older and wiser, then a lot worldlier, just how I wanted.

Oh, how you've surprised me throughout my life, dear Mum. Apart from having one of the best belly-laughs I've known, you have shown me how much a mother can love her children. You have displayed strength and courage when I least expected it and shown me how kind a person can be. Love, strength, courage and kindness, they are the attributes you have and the attributes which I'd like to think I absorbed from you. This is what I hope to give to my children. You are forever in my heart, with love.

EPILOGUE

To every woman for whom relinquishing their babies was their path, chosen or coerced; I stand with you.

To everyone who stood up, stood out and took risks to advocate and support unmarried women and the pursuit of equality and fertility rights; I applaud you.

To the couples who waited patiently for their babies to arrive into their arms, who grew their children with unconditional love, commitment and kindness; I love you.

To the people who upheld government policies of the times, in children's services, hospitals, charities and churches of the time, in ignorance and with good intentions; I excuse you.

To the men who abandoned their pregnant girlfriends because of familial and societal pressures of the day; I think I understand.

To the men who will never read this, the ones who never knew they had become fathers because of the shame or incapacity of those women to disclose the truth; I am sorry you will never know what you missed.

To the children who grew up not knowing their truth, who searched and found and lost; I am you.

Acknowledgements

My thanks to:
Georgina Naidu, Yoni Prior, Paul Harris, Dr Natasha Andreadis, Dom Harden, Rebecca Thorpe, Rebecca Gerret-Magee, Paola Balla, Catherine Deveny, Michael Hyde, Kim Clarke, Ashley Carr, Rebecca Gelsi, Maggie Sakko, Cheryl Johnstone, Sharone Ciancio, Mariella Camilleri, Ann-Maree Noble, Tim Willis, Kerrie, Angelo, Chris, Joanna, Janis Lesinskis, Anne Maree Rourke, Cath Pirret, Gionni DiGravio, Vicki Bright, Alex Couley, Andrew Ingram, Angus Ingram, Brigit Ingram, Tracy Main, Emma Workman, Bronwyn McGarry, Rebecca Barnard, Sharon Bailey, Bonnie Griffin, Simone Hatherly, Mark Hanlon, Catherine Kavanagh, Dr Ann Hardy, Louise O'Day, Jodie Morgan, Dagmar Anderson, Lisa Williams, Michelle Taylor, Nanette Shone, Karen Jackson, Sarah Tartakover, Peta Oates, Nellie Flagg, Michele Leonard, Deb Chapman, Jodie Scott, Roger Gierson, Rocco, Adriana and Louisa from Rocco's Deli.

Posthumous gratitude to Hugh Oates, Teddie Oates and Enid McGarry.

Love and gratitude to my family: Mum, Dad, Jeff, Nina, Neil, Jill, Nick, Rui, Marc, Seda, Jeremy, Emma, Ruby, Luke, Brooke, Nathan, Adele, Lillian, Lachlan, Shirl, Maggie, Ian and my darling hearts Andrew, Angus and Brigit.

At the time of going to print my search for my biological father continues. The fractured relationships with my aunts Bronwyn and Barbara will continue to heal. I have been estranged from Madeline from around a year before Ann's death. I am grateful for the continued support, love and understanding of Silvio, Maxine and Ben.

www.ingramcontent.com/pod-product-compliance
Lightning Source LLC
Chambersburg PA
CBHW070248010526
44107CB00056B/2384